diabetic LIVING® Everyday COOKING

VOLUME 8

DIABETIC LIVING® EVERYDAY COOKING
IS PART OF A BOOK SERIES PUBLISHED BY
BETTER HOMES AND GARDENS SPECIAL
INTEREST MEDIA, DES MOINES, IOWA

Pretzel-Pistachio-
Crusted Tofu Salad
recipe on page 56

Prepare good-for-you meals your family will love.

The recipes in this new volume of *Diabetic Living®* *Everyday Cooking* feature fresh, quality ingredients and the most healthful cooking techniques. You will use this collection often for nutritious meals and snacks that fit into a diabetes meal plan and appeal to the whole family.

All of the recipes are dietitian-approved and live up to the stringent Better Homes and Gardens® Test Kitchen seal of approval. That means they are accurate, easy to prepare, and guaranteed to taste great. Each one has a nutritional profile that fits a healthful diet for people with diabetes. The nutritional analysis after each one highlights carbohydrate, fiber, and sugars and lists diabetic exchanges to help keep you on track.

Turn to this cookbook when you're looking for something nutritious and tasty to prepare for breakfast, lunch, and dinner. You'll also find satisfying snacks to help keep blood sugars in check throughout the day. And it includes a dessert section! Look for great ideas for delicious treats that won't bankrupt your carbohydrate budget.

Make your everyday cooking special every day!

30

98

132

ON THE COVER:

Blueberry Buckwheat Pancakes recipe on page 113

Photographer: Jason Donnelly

diabetic LIVING® **Everyday COOKING** VOLUME 8

CONSUMER MARKETING

Vice President, Consumer Marketing	JANET DONNELLY
Consumer Marketing Product Director	HEATHER SORENSEN
Consumer Marketing Product Manager	WENDY MERICAL
Business Director	RON CLINGMAN
Production Manager	AL RODRUCK
Contributing Project Manager	SHELLI McCONNELL, PURPLE PEAR PUBLISHING, INC.
Contributing Photographer	JASON DONNELLY
Contributing Food Stylist	JENNIFER PETERSON
Test Kitchen Director	LYNN BLANCHARD
Test Kitchen Product Supervisor	CARLA CHRISTIAN, RD, LD
Editorial Assistants	LORI EGGERS, MARLENE TODD

SPECIAL INTEREST MEDIA

Group Editorial Leader	DOUG KOUMA
Art Director	GENE RAUCH

DIABETIC LIVING® MAGAZINE

Senior Editor	MARTHA MILLER JOHNSON
Art Director	MICHELLE BILYEU
Senior Associate Editor	JESSIE SHAFER
Assistant Art Director	NIKKI SANDERS

MEREDITH NATIONAL MEDIA GROUP

President **TOM HARTY**

meredith

Chairman and Chief Executive Officer **STEPHEN M. LACY**

Vice Chairman **MELL MEREDITH FRAZIER**

In Memoriam — E.T. MEREDITH III (1933-2003)

Diabetic Living® Everyday Cooking **is part of a series published by Meredith Corp.,** 1716 Locust St., Des Moines, IA 50309-3023.

If you have comments or questions about the editorial material in *Diabetic Living® Everyday Cooking,* write to the editor of *Diabetic Living* magazine, Meredith Corp., 1716 Locust St., Des Moines, IA 50309-3023. Send an e-mail to *diabeticlivingmeredith.com* or call 800/678-2651. magazine is available by subscription or on the newsstand. To order a subscription to magazine, go to *DiabeticLivingOnline.com*

contents

Southwestern Cherry-
Oat Chicken Sandwiches
recipe on page 75

1

family-pleasing
dinners

Pizza, stir-fries, quick pasta tosses, and casseroles are some

of the healthful yet satisfying dinners that are easy to serve

during the week or for a special weekend meal. Slimmed-down

versions of family favorites and new introductions to the dinner

table are sure to keep the whole family happy.

Mediterranean Couscous and Beef

Israeli couscous is larger and rounder than regular couscous. If you can't find it, substitute any very small pasta, such as orzo.

SERVINGS 4 (3½ ounces cooked beef and ½ cup couscous mixture each)
CARB. PER SERVING 26 g
PREP 35 minutes BROIL 12 minutes

¾ cup Israeli (pearl) couscous

Nonstick cooking spray

1 pound beef flank steak

½ teaspoon black pepper

¼ teaspoon salt

5 tablespoons salt-free lemon-herb-peppercorn flavor marinade, such as Mrs. Dash brand

1 cup water

2 medium red and/or yellow tomatoes, seeded and coarsely chopped

¼ cup crumbled reduced-fat feta cheese (1 ounce)

1 Heat a dry medium saucepan over medium-low heat. Add couscous to hot saucepan; toast couscous for 8 to 10 minutes or until golden brown, stirring frequently. Remove couscous from saucepan.

2 Meanwhile, preheat broiler. Lightly coat the unheated rack of a broiler pan with cooking spray. Trim fat from beef. Season beef with ¼ teaspoon of the pepper and ⅛ teaspoon of the salt. Pour 1 tablespoon of the marinade into a custard cup; set aside the remaining 4 tablespoons marinade. Brush the 1 tablespoon marinade onto beef. Place beef on the prepared rack. Broil 4 to 5 inches from the heat until desired doneness, turning once; allow 12 to 14 minutes for medium.

3 In the same medium saucepan combine the water, the remaining ¼ teaspoon pepper, and the remaining ⅛ teaspoon salt; bring to boiling. Stir in couscous; return to boiling and reduce heat. Simmer, covered, for 7 minutes. Stir in the reserved 4 tablespoons marinade, the tomatoes, and 2 tablespoons of the feta cheese. Cook for 1 to 2 minutes more or until couscous and tomatoes are tender.

4 To serve, thinly slice beef across the grain; serve over couscous mixture. Sprinkle with the remaining 2 tablespoons feta cheese.

PER SERVING: 317 cal., 10 g total fat (3 g sat. fat), 73 mg chol., 330 mg sodium, 26 g carb. (2 g fiber, 3 g sugars), 30 g pro. Exchanges: 0.5 vegetable, 1.5 starch, 3.5 lean meat, 0.5 fat.

Steaks with Strawberry-Wine Sauce

Reducing wine and balsamic vinegar, then combining the mixture with strawberries produces a complex sweet and tangy sauce.

SERVINGS 4 (4 ounces cooked beef, 1/3 cup sauce, and 5 strawberries each)
CARB. PER SERVING 15 g or 13 g
PREP 35 minutes   GRILL 9 minutes

- 2   8- to 10-ounce boneless beef top loin steaks or boneless beef chuck top blade (flat iron) steaks, cut 3/4 inch thick
- 1/2   teaspoon salt
- 1/2   teaspoon cracked black pepper or freshly ground black pepper
- 20   medium fresh strawberries
  Nonstick cooking spray
- 2   small shallots, thinly sliced
- 1/2   cup Cabernet wine, pomegranate juice, or low-calorie cranberry juice*
- 2   small sprigs fresh rosemary
- 2   tablespoons balsamic vinegar
- 2   teaspoons sugar**
- 1 1/2   cups fresh strawberries, hulled and quartered
  Chopped green onions (optional)

PER SERVING: 237 cal., 6 g total fat (2 g sat. fat), 69 mg chol., 360 mg sodium, 15 g carb. (3 g fiber, 10 g sugars), 26 g pro. Exchanges: 1 fruit, 3.5 lean meat.

PER SERVING WITH SUBSTITUTE: Same as above, except 230 cal., 13 g carb. (8 g sugars).

1 Trim fat from beef steaks. Cut each steak in half. Sprinkle steaks with the salt and pepper. On four 10-inch skewers, thread the 20 strawberries, leaving 1/4 inch between strawberries. Set aside.

2 For sauce, coat a medium nonstick skillet with cooking spray. Heat skillet over medium heat. Add shallots; cook for 4 to 5 minutes or just until tender, stirring occasionally. Remove from heat; carefully add wine to the skillet. Add rosemary sprigs. Return to medium heat. Cook, uncovered, for 3 to 4 minutes or until wine is reduced by about half. Stir in vinegar and sugar. Add the quartered strawberries. Cook for 3 to 4 minutes more or just until strawberries are softened, stirring occasionally. Remove and discard rosemary sprigs. Cover sauce; keep warm.

3 For a charcoal or gas grill, grill steaks on the rack of a covered grill directly over medium heat until desired doneness. Allow 9 to 11 minutes for medium rare (145°F) or 11 to 13 minutes for medium (160°F), turning once halfway through grilling time. When you turn the steaks, add strawberry skewers to grill rack. Grill skewers for 3 to 4 minutes or until strawberries are warm, turning once.

4 Divide steak portions and strawberry skewers among four serving plates. Spoon sauce over steak. If desired, sprinkle with green onions.

*TEST KITCHEN TIP: If using pomegranate juice or cranberry juice, omit the sugar.

**SUGAR SUBSTITUTES: Choose Splenda Granular or Sweet'N Low bulk or packets. Follow package directions to use product amount equivalent to 2 teaspoons sugar.

Greek Beef Kabobs

The meat and vegetables for these kabobs are tossed in an "instant marinade" for quick flavor. Serve them with zesty Cucumber Salad.

SERVINGS 4 (1 skewer and $^3/_4$ cup salad each)
CARB. PER SERVING 12 g
PREP 45 minutes GRILL 10 minutes

- 2 tablespoons balsamic vinegar
- 2 teaspoons olive oil
- 2 teaspoons finely shredded lemon peel
- 1 teaspoon dried oregano, crushed
- 2 cloves garlic, minced
- $^1/_4$ teaspoon salt
- $^1/_4$ teaspoon black pepper
- 1 pound beef top sirloin steak
- 1 large red sweet pepper, cut into $1^1/_2$-inch pieces
- 1 medium onion, halved crosswise and cut into wedges
- 1 recipe Cucumber Salad

1 In a shallow dish whisk together the vinegar, oil, lemon peel, oregano, garlic, salt, and black pepper. Trim fat from beef. Cut meat into $1^1/_2$-inch pieces. Add meat, sweet pepper, and onion to vinegar mixture; toss to coat. On four 10-inch skewers,* alternately thread meat, sweet pepper, and onion, leaving $^1/_4$ inch between pieces.

2 For a charcoal or gas grill, grill kabobs on the rack of an uncovered grill directly over medium heat for 10 to 12 minutes or until meat reaches desired doneness, turning once halfway through grilling. Serve with Cucumber Salad.

CUCUMBER SALAD: In a medium bowl stir together $^1/_2$ cup plain fat-free Greek yogurt; 2 cloves garlic, minced; $^1/_2$ teaspoon finely shredded lemon peel; $^1/_2$ teaspoon dried dill weed; $^1/_4$ teaspoon salt; and dash cayenne pepper. Stir in 1 large cucumber, thinly sliced (3 cups) and $^1/_2$ cup thinly slivered red onion.

*TEST KITCHEN TIP: If using wooden skewers, soak in enough water to cover for 30 minutes; drain before using.

PER SERVING: 278 cal., 12 g total fat (4 g sat. fat), 63 mg chol., 373 mg sodium, 12 g carb. (2 g fiber, 6 g sugars), 28 g pro. Exchanges: 1.5 vegetable, 0.5 carb., 3.5 lean meat, 1 fat.

12 grams carb.

Pork Tacos with Peach Salsa

Make this when peaches or nectarines are at their peak of freshness. Fresh mangoes make a good stand-in.

SERVINGS 4 (2 tacos each)
CARB. PER SERVING 25 g
PREP 20 minutes
GRILL 25 minutes
STAND 3 minutes

- 1 1-pound pork tenderloin
- 1 teaspoon salt-free fiesta lime seasoning blend, such as Mrs. Dash brand
- ¼ teaspoon salt
- 2 peaches, halved and pitted
- ½ cup finely chopped red onion (1 medium)
- ½ of a fresh jalapeño chile pepper, seeded and chopped (see tip, *page 23*)
- ¼ cup snipped fresh cilantro
- 1 tablespoon lime juice
- ¼ teaspoon salt
- 8 5½- to 6-inch corn tortillas, warmed

PER SERVING: 238 cal., 3 g total fat (1 g sat. fat), 73 mg chol., 346 mg sodium, 25 g carb. (4 g fiber, 9 g sugars), 27 g pro. Exchanges: 0.5 fruit, 1 starch, 3.5 lean meat.

1 Trim fat from pork. Sprinkle pork with fiesta lime seasoning blend and the ¼ teaspoon salt. For a charcoal grill, arrange medium coals on one side of the grill. Place a drip pan on the other side of the grill. Place pork on the greased grill rack over the drip pan. Cover and grill for 25 to 30 minutes or until an instant-read thermometer inserted in center of pork registers 145°F.

2 Meanwhile, place peach halves, pitted sides down, on the greased grill rack directly over the coals. Cover and grill about 6 minutes or until tender and lightly browned, turning once. (For a gas grill, preheat grill. Reduce heat to medium. Adjust for indirect cooking. Place meat on greased grill rack over burner that is off. Place peaches on greased grill rack over burner that is on. Grill as above.) Remove pork from grill. Cover with foil and let stand for 3 minutes. Slice pork very thin.

3 Coarsely chop peaches. In a small bowl combine peaches, red onion, chile pepper, cilantro, lime juice, and the ¼ teaspoon salt. Serve pork and peach salsa in warmed tortillas.

Mustard Pork with Rhubarb Sauce

This springtime dish is special enough for serving to guests but easy enough to make during the week.

SERVINGS 8 (4 ounces cooked meat and about 2 tablespoons sauce each)
CARB. PER SERVING 12 g
PREP 30 minutes **ROAST** 55 minutes at 350°F **STAND** 3 minutes

- 1 2- to 2½-pound boneless pork top loin roast (single loin)
- ¼ cup Dijon-style mustard
- 6 to 12 cloves garlic, minced
- 1 tablespoon snipped fresh rosemary
- ½ teaspoon salt
- ¼ teaspoon black pepper
- 3 cups fresh or frozen sliced rhubarb (about 1 pound)
- ⅓ to ½ cup sugar*
- ⅓ cup orange juice
- 1 tablespoon cider vinegar

1 Preheat oven to 350°F. Trim fat from meat. Score top and bottom of meat in a diamond pattern by making shallow diagonal cuts at 1-inch intervals. In a small bowl combine mustard, garlic, rosemary, salt, and pepper. Spread mixture evenly over all sides of meat.

2 Place meat on a rack in a shallow roasting pan. Roast for 55 to 75 minutes or until an instant-read thermometer inserted in the center of meat registers 145°F. Transfer meat to a cutting board. Cover with foil and let stand for 3 minutes.

3 Meanwhile, for rhubarb sauce, in a medium saucepan combine rhubarb, sugar, orange juice, and vinegar. Bring to boiling; reduce heat. Simmer, covered, about 15 minutes or until rhubarb is very tender.

4 To serve, slice the meat and top each serving with 2 tablespoons warm rhubarb sauce. Pass the remaining sauce.

GRILLING DIRECTIONS: For a charcoal grill, arrange medium-hot coals around a drip pan. Test for medium heat above pan. Place meat on grill rack over drip pan. Cover and grill for 50 to 70 minutes or until an instant-read thermometer inserted in the center of meat registers 145°F. (For a gas grill, preheat grill. Reduce heat to medium. Adjust for indirect cooking. Grill as above, except place meat on a rack in a shallow roasting pan; place pan on grill rack.) Remove meat from grill. Cover with foil and let stand for 3 minutes.

*SUGAR SUBSTITUTES: We do not recommend using a sugar substitute for this recipe.

PER SERVING: 175 cal., 4 g total fat (1 g sat. fat), 60 mg chol., 358 mg sodium, 12 g carb. (1 g fiber, 10 g sugars), 22 g pro. Exchanges: 0.5 vegetable, 0.5 carb., 3 lean meat.

Spicy Stir-Fried Pork with Bok Choy

This veggie-loaded stir-fry is filling and fast. It's perfect for a quick weeknight meal.

SERVINGS 4 (1 cup pork-vegetable mixture and $^1/_2$ cup rice each)
CARB. PER SERVING 33 g
START TO FINISH 20 minutes

1 tablespoon canola oil

4 cups coarsely shredded bok choy

1$^1/_2$ cups packaged shredded carrots

1 onion, cut into thin wedges ($^1/_2$ cup)

$^1/_4$ teaspoon crushed red pepper

1 pound boneless pork loin, cut into bite-size strips

1 tablespoon reduced-sodium soy sauce

1 tablespoon rice vinegar

1 tablespoon grated fresh ginger

2 cloves garlic, minced

2 to 3 teaspoons Asian chili sauce (Sriracha sauce)

1 teaspoon toasted sesame oil

2 cups hot cooked brown rice

2 tablespoons broken cashews

PER SERVING: 361 cal., 12 g total fat (2 g sat. fat), 78 mg chol., 309 mg sodium, 33 g carb. (4 g fiber, 5 g sugars), 30 g pro. Exchanges: 1.5 vegetable, 1.5 starch, 3 lean meat, 1 fat.

1 Heat a wok or very large skillet over medium-high heat. Add $^1/_2$ tablespoon of the oil and swirl to coat skillet. Add bok choy, carrots, onion, and crushed red pepper. Stir-fry for 2 to 3 minutes or until vegetables are crisp-tender. Remove vegetables from wok; set aside.

2 Add the remaining $^1/_2$ tablespoon oil to the wok or skillet. Add the pork strips in a single layer. Let cook, without stirring, for 1 minute to sear. Stir-fry pork for 3 to 4 minutes or until no longer pink and liquid is almost evaporated. Add the soy sauce, vinegar, ginger, and garlic. Stir-fry for 1 minute. Return the vegetables to the wok and add the chili sauce and sesame oil. Toss to combine. Serve mixture over brown rice. Sprinkle with cashews.

Pineapple, Bacon, and Kale Pizza

Instead of loading your pizza with meats and cheese, use them sparingly. This pizza boasts a generous helping of beautiful, nutritious greens.

SERVINGS 4 (2 slices pizza each)
CARB. PER SERVING 40 g
START TO FINISH 20 minutes

1 12-inch 100% whole wheat thin pizza crust, such as Boboli brand

⅓ cup pizza sauce

¾ cup chopped kale

½ cup shredded part-skim mozzarella cheese (2 ounces)

⅓ cup canned pineapple chunks (juice pack), drained and coarsely chopped

4 slices lower-sodium and less-fat bacon, crisp-cooked and coarsely chopped

1 Preheat oven to 450°F. Place pizza crust on a 12-inch pizza pan or a baking sheet. Bake for 8 minutes. Spread pizza sauce on crust. Top with chopped kale, mozzarella cheese, pineapple, and bacon. Bake for 5 to 8 minutes more or until crust is golden brown and cheese is melted. Cut into eight slices.

PER SERVING: 276 cal., 8 g total fat (4 g sat. fat), 12 mg chol., 551 mg sodium, 40 g carb. (7 g fiber, 7 g sugars), 14 g pro. Exchanges: 1 vegetable, 2 starch, 1.5 medium-fat meat.

Bourbon Chicken Skewers

Bourbon adds a hint of its unique flavor to this rich and tangy sauce. Cook sauce until it is thick enough to cling on the skewers.

SERVINGS 4 (2 skewers each)
CARB. PER SERVING 18 g or 14 g
PREP 25 minutes GRILL 10 minutes

- $^1/_3$ cup bottled barbecue sauce
- 2 tablespoons packed brown sugar*
- 2 tablespoons bourbon or apple juice
- 1 tablespoon reduced-sodium soy sauce
- 1 teaspoon cider vinegar
- $^1/_8$ teaspoon salt
- 1 pound skinless, boneless chicken thighs, cut into 1-inch chunks
- 1 medium zucchini, cut into 1-inch-thick pieces
- 4 green onions, cut into 2-inch-long pieces

PER SERVING: 225 cal., 5 g total fat (1 g sat. fat), 108 mg chol., 510 mg sodium, 18 g carb. (1 g fiber, 15 g sugars), 23 g pro. Exchanges: 1.5 vegetable, 0.5 carb., 3 lean meat.

PER SERVING WITH SUBSTITUTE: Same as above, except 213 cal., 14 g carb. (11 g sugars).

1 For bourbon sauce, in a small saucepan combine barbecue sauce, brown sugar, bourbon, soy sauce, cider vinegar, and salt. Bring to boiling; reduce heat. Simmer, uncovered, for 3 to 5 minutes or until thickened.

2 On eight 8- to 10-inch skewers,** alternately thread chicken, zucchini, and green onions, leaving $^1/_4$ inch between pieces. Brush with bourbon sauce. For a charcoal or gas grill, grill skewers on the rack of a covered grill directly over medium heat for 5 minutes. Turn and brush with bourbon sauce; discard any remaining sauce. Grill for 5 to 7 minutes more or until chicken is no longer pink, turning occasionally.

*SUGAR SUBSTITUTES: Choose Splenda Brown Sugar Blend for Baking. Follow package directions to use product amount equivalent to 2 tablespoons brown sugar.

**TEST KITCHEN TIP: If using wooden skewers, soak in enough water to cover for 30 minutes; drain before using.

Chicken Enchilada Muffins

Skip the tortillas with these enchiladas. Sharp cheddar cheese in the muffins contributes a rich, cheesy flavor with less fat.

》》 SERVINGS 6 (1 muffin plus $^2/_3$ cup chicken mixture each)
CARB. PER SERVING 30 g or 29 g
PREP 30 minutes BAKE 18 minutes at 400°F COOL 5 minutes

1 cup yellow cornmeal
$^3/_4$ cup whole wheat flour
3 tablespoons sugar*
2 teaspoons baking powder
1 6-ounce carton plain fat-free Greek yogurt
$^1/_2$ cup fat-free milk
2 eggs
2 tablespoons canola oil
$^1/_2$ cup shredded sharp cheddar cheese (2 ounces)
1 4-ounce can diced green chile peppers, drained
20 ounces skinless, boneless chicken breast halves and/or thighs, coarsely chopped
1 cup chopped onion (1 large)
2 cloves garlic, minced
1 14.5-ounce can no-salt-added petite diced tomatoes, undrained
1 8-ounce can no-salt-added tomato sauce
1 teaspoon ground cumin
$^1/_2$ teaspoon salt
$^1/_2$ teaspoon dried basil, crushed
$^1/_2$ teaspoon dried oregano, crushed
1 avocado, halved, seeded, peeled, and coarsely chopped

1 | Preheat oven to 400°F. Generously coat twelve $2^1/_2$-inch muffin cups with *nonstick cooking spray*. Wipe each cup with a paper towel to ensure cups are evenly coated.

2 | In a medium bowl stir together cornmeal, flour, sugar, and baking powder; set aside. In another medium bowl whisk together yogurt, milk, eggs, and oil. Stir in cheese and chile peppers. Add milk mixture all at once to the cornmeal mixture. Stir just until moistened. Spoon batter into prepared muffin cups, filling each about two-thirds full. Bake for 18 to 20 minutes or until golden brown and a wooden toothpick inserted in centers comes out clean. Cool in muffin cups on a wire rack for 5 minutes. Run a small knife around the edge of each cup; remove muffins from cups. Set aside six of the muffins to top with chicken mixture. (Completely cool the remaining six muffins; store in an airtight container for up to 3 days in the refrigerator or for up to 1 month in the freezer. If frozen, thaw before using.)

3 | Meanwhile, coat a large nonstick skillet with cooking spray. Preheat over medium-high heat. Add chicken to hot skillet; cook for 8 to 10 minutes or until no longer pink. Remove chicken with a slotted spoon; set aside and keep warm. Add onion and garlic to the same skillet; cook and stir about 5 minutes or until tender. Add tomatoes, tomato sauce, cumin, salt, basil, and oregano. Bring to boiling; reduce heat. Simmer, uncovered, for 5 to 10 minutes or until slightly thickened. Stir in chicken. Cook and stir just until chicken is heated through.

4 | To serve, split each of the six reserved muffins and top with chicken mixture. Top with chopped avocado. If desired, garnish with *cracked black pepper*.

*SUGAR SUBSTITUTES: Choose from Splenda Sugar Blend or C&H Light Sugar Blend. Follow package directions to use product amount equivalent to 3 tablespoons sugar.

PER SERVING: 331 cal., 12 g total fat (3 g sat. fat), 111 mg chol., 486 mg sodium, 30 g carb. (5 g fiber, 10 g sugars), 27 g pro. Exchanges: 1 vegetable, 1.5 starch, 3 lean meat, 1 fat.

PER SERVING WITH SUBSTITUTE: Same as above, except 326 cal., 29 g carb. (8 g sugars).

Roasted Mediterranean Chicken

Mediterranean cooking is all about using the best fresh ingredients available. This dish is loaded with fresh springtime flavors.

SERVINGS 4 (2 cups each)
CARB. PER SERVING 27 g
PREP 25 minutes ROAST 45 minutes at 425°F

- 2 tablespoons snipped fresh parsley
- 1 tablespoon snipped fresh oregano
- 1 tablespoon snipped fresh basil
- 1 teaspoon snipped fresh rosemary
- 1/4 teaspoon salt
- 1/4 teaspoon black pepper
- 1 1/2 pounds skinless, boneless chicken thighs or breasts
- 8 ounces fresh mushrooms, sliced
- 1 red onion, sliced
- 1/2 cup chopped red and/or green sweet pepper
- 2 cloves garlic, minced
- 1 tablespoon olive oil
- 1 pound fresh asparagus spears, trimmed and cut into 2- to 3-inch pieces
- 1 15- to 16-ounce can cannellini beans (white kidney beans), rinsed and drained
- 1 cup red and/or yellow cherry tomatoes
- 10 pitted Kalamata olives
- 2 tablespoons balsamic vinegar

PER SERVING: 360 cal., 12 g total fat (2 g sat. fat), 161 mg chol., 524 mg sodium, 27 g carb. (9 g fiber, 6 g sugars), 43 g pro. Exchanges: 2 vegetable, 1 starch, 5 lean meat, 0.5 fat.

1 Preheat oven to 425°F. Line two 15x10x1-inch baking pans with foil; set aside. In a small bowl combine parsley, oregano, basil, rosemary, salt, and black pepper. Place chicken on one of the prepared pans. Sprinkle with half of the herb mixture. In a large bowl combine mushrooms, onion, sweet pepper, and garlic. Drizzle with oil; toss to coat. Place mushroom mixture on the other prepared baking pan.

2 Roast chicken and vegetables for 30 minutes, stirring vegetable mixture once. If chicken is tender and no longer pink (at least 170°F), remove from oven and cover to keep warm; if not, continue roasting until done. Add asparagus, beans, tomatoes, olives, balsamic vinegar, and the remaining herb mixture to the mushroom mixture in the other baking pan; stir to combine. Continue to roast the vegetable mixture about 15 minutes more or until asparagus is crisp-tender.

3 To serve, cut chicken into bite-size pieces; combine with roasted vegetables.

Parmesan Chicken on Bruschetta-Style Vegetables

Save the bread for another time. The flavors of bruschetta make this chicken Parmesan dance.

>> SERVINGS 4 (1 chicken breast half and 1 cup tomato mixture each)
CARB. PER SERVING 16 g
PREP 20 minutes BAKE 30 minutes at 375°F

- ½ cup panko bread crumbs
- 2 tablespoons grated Parmesan cheese
- ½ teaspoon dried Italian seasoning, crushed
- 1 egg white
- 4 5-ounce skinless, boneless chicken breast halves (1¼ pounds total)
- Nonstick cooking spray
- 1 tablespoon olive oil
- ½ cup finely chopped onion (1 medium)
- 3 cups fresh spinach leaves
- 1½ cups sliced fresh mushrooms (4 ounces)
- 2 to 3 cloves garlic, minced
- 3 cups peeled, seeded, and chopped tomatoes, well drained (6 medium)
- 2 tablespoons snipped fresh basil
- 1 tablespoon balsamic vinegar
- ¼ teaspoon salt
- ¼ teaspoon black pepper
- Snipped fresh parsley (optional)

PER SERVING: 288 cal., 8 g total fat (2 g sat. fat), 93 mg chol., 395 mg sodium, 16 g carb. (4 g fiber, 6 g sugars), 36 g pro. Exchanges: 2 vegetable, 0.5 starch, 4 lean meat, 0.5 fat.

1 | Preheat oven to 375°F. Place a rack in a shallow baking pan; set aside. In a shallow bowl combine bread crumbs, cheese, and Italian seasoning. In another shallow bowl beat egg white with a fork. Dip chicken into egg white, then into crumb mixture, turning to coat. Arrange chicken in the prepared baking pan. Lightly coat tops of chicken pieces with cooking spray. Bake about 30 minutes or until chicken is no longer pink (165°F) and coating is crisp. If desired, for better browning, turn the broiler on for the last 2 to 3 minutes of cooking.

2 | Meanwhile, in a very large nonstick skillet heat oil over medium-high heat. Add onion; cook about 3 minutes or until tender, stirring occasionally. Add spinach, mushrooms, and garlic. Cook about 5 minutes or until spinach is wilted, mushrooms are tender, and liquid is evaporated, stirring occasionally. Remove from heat. Stir in tomatoes, basil, vinegar, salt, and pepper. Serve chicken on top of tomato mixture. If desired, sprinkle with parsley.

Coconut Lime Chicken Pasta

Coconut milk and Greek yogurt give this Thai-style dish a creamy tang. Crushed red pepper and lime juice provide the zing.

SERVINGS 4 (1¼ cups each)
CARB. PER SERVING 27 g
START TO FINISH 40 minutes

- 4 ounces dried whole wheat linguine or spaghetti
- 1 tablespoon olive oil
- 3 shallots, finely chopped (6 tablespoons)
- 2 large cloves garlic, minced
- ¼ teaspoon crushed red pepper
- 1 pound skinless, boneless chicken breast halves, cut into bite-size strips
- ¼ teaspoon coarsely ground black pepper
- 2 tablespoons lime juice
- 1 cup unsweetened light coconut milk
- ¼ cup plain low-fat Greek yogurt
- 1 tablespoon finely shredded lime peel
- ½ cup coarsely snipped fresh cilantro
- Fresh cilantro sprigs (optional)
- Lime wedges (optional)

1 | Cook pasta according to package directions, omitting any salt. Drain pasta; set aside.

2 | Meanwhile, in a very large nonstick skillet heat 2 teaspoons of the oil over medium-high heat. Add shallots, garlic, and crushed red pepper; cook for 30 seconds. Sprinkle chicken breast strips with black pepper; add to skillet. Cook and stir until chicken is no longer pink. Using a slotted spoon, transfer chicken to a plate; cover and keep warm.

3 | Whisk the remaining 1 teaspoon oil and the lime juice into the skillet, using a wooden spoon to scrape up any browned bits from bottom of the skillet. Add cooked pasta; toss to coat. In a small bowl whisk together coconut milk, yogurt, and lime peel; add to the skillet. Cook and stir for 2 minutes. Stir in ¼ cup of the snipped cilantro and the cooked chicken. Heat through. Sprinkle with the remaining ¼ cup snipped cilantro. If desired, garnish with cilantro sprigs and/or lime wedges.

30 grams pro.

PER SERVING: 323 cal., 11 g total fat (4 g sat. fat), 73 mg chol., 125 mg sodium, 27 g carb. (4 g fiber, 4 g sugars), 30 g pro. Exchanges: 1 vegetable, 1.5 starch, 3.5 lean meat, 0.5 fat.

QUICK TIP

Save the leftover coconut milk in the refrigerator and use it in smoothies. It can help stabilize blood sugar and combat inflammation.

Chicken and Broccolini Cavatelli

Broccolini is a cross between broccoli and Chinese kale. Use either broccoli or kale as a substitute if you can't find it.

>> SERVINGS 6 (1 cup each)
CARB. PER SERVING 33 g
PREP 40 minutes   ROAST 20 minutes at 400°F

- 1 whole bulb garlic
- 3 teaspoons olive oil
- 6 ounces dried cavatelli pasta
- 3 cups Broccolini spears (about 8 ounces)
- 2 ounces pancetta, finely chopped
- 1 pound skinless, boneless chicken breast halves, cut into 1$\frac{1}{2}$- to 2-inch pieces
- 3 tablespoons light butter with canola oil
- 3 tablespoons flour
- 2 tablespoons snipped fresh chives
- $\frac{1}{2}$ teaspoon salt
- $\frac{1}{4}$ teaspoon black pepper
- 1 cup fat-free milk
- $\frac{1}{2}$ cup evaporated fat-free milk
- 2 tablespoons freshly grated Parmesan cheese

Snipped fresh chives

PER SERVING: 343 cal., 10 g total fat (3 g sat. fat), 57 mg chol., 464 mg sodium, 33 g carb. (2 g fiber, 7 g sugars), 27 g pro. Exchanges: 1 vegetable, 2 starch, 3 lean meat, 1.5 fat.

1 Preheat oven to 400°F. Cut off the top $\frac{1}{2}$ inch of the garlic bulb to expose ends of individual cloves. Leaving bulb whole, remove any loose papery outer layers. Place bulb, cut end up, on a double thickness of foil. Drizzle bulb with 1 teaspoon of the olive oil. Bring foil up around bulb and fold edges together to loosely enclose. Roast for 20 to 25 minutes or until garlic feels soft when squeezed. Let the garlic bulb cool. Squeeze garlic from skins into a small bowl; mash with a fork. Set aside.

2 Meanwhile, cook pasta according to package directions, adding Broccolini for the last 4 minutes of cooking. Drain, reserving $\frac{1}{2}$ cup of the pasta cooking liquid. Set pasta, Broccolini, and reserved cooking liquid aside.

3 In a 6-quart Dutch oven heat the remaining 2 teaspoons olive oil over medium heat. Add pancetta; cook for 5 to 7 minutes or until crisp. Remove pancetta from Dutch oven; set aside. Add chicken pieces to Dutch oven. Cook for 7 to 8 minutes or until chicken is no longer pink (165°F). Remove from Dutch oven; set aside.

4 In the same Dutch oven melt light butter over medium heat. Whisk in the mashed garlic, the flour, the 2 tablespoons chives, the salt, and pepper until combined. Add milk and evaporated milk, whisking until smooth. Cook and stir the mixture until thickened and bubbly. Add Parmesan cheese, cooked chicken, cooked pasta, and cooked Broccolini; toss to combine. Add enough of the reserved pasta cooking liquid to reach desired consistency. Top with crispy pancetta and additional chives.

Cashew-Cilantro Pesto with Veggie Noodles

Skip the pasta and make thinly shaved vegetables as the base for this "noodle" dish. Or use a spiral slicer to turn veggies into long strands.

SERVINGS 5 (1 cup each)
CARB. PER SERVING 26 g
START TO FINISH 30 minutes

- 1 English cucumber, peeled (about 7 ounces)
- 1 daikon radish, peeled (about 12 ounces)
- 3 carrots (about 3$\frac{1}{2}$ ounces)
- 2 cups thinly sliced savoy cabbage
- $\frac{1}{2}$ teaspoon kosher salt
- 1 cup raw cashews
- $\frac{3}{4}$ cup snipped fresh cilantro
- 3 green onions, chopped
- $\frac{1}{2}$ cup lime juice
- 2 tablespoons raw agave nectar
- 1 fresh jalapeño chile pepper, seeded and finely chopped (about 1$\frac{1}{2}$ tablespoons)*
- 1 tablespoon tamari sauce
- 2 teaspoons grated fresh ginger
- 2 teaspoons sesame oil
- 3 cloves garlic

1 | Using a vegetable peeler, cut the cucumber, daikon radish, and carrots lengthwise into long julienne noodles or ribbons. In a very large bowl toss together the vegetable noodles, cabbage, and kosher salt. Set aside while preparing the pesto. Reserve any liquid that is released from the vegetables as they stand.

2 | For pesto, in a food processor or blender combine cashews, $\frac{1}{2}$ cup of the cilantro, the green onions, lime juice, agave nectar, chile pepper, tamari sauce, ginger, sesame oil, and garlic. Cover and blend or process until smooth. If necessary, add some of the liquid from the salted vegetables or a little water to thin mixture to a sauce consistency.

3 | Toss the vegetable noodles with the pesto; sprinkle with the remaining $\frac{1}{4}$ cup cilantro.

*TEST KITCHEN TIP: Because chile peppers contain volatile oils that can burn your skin and eyes, avoid direct contact with them as much as possible. When working with chile peppers, wear plastic or rubber gloves. If your bare hands do touch the peppers, wash your hands and nails well with soap and warm water.

PER SERVING: 248 cal., 15 g total fat (3 g sat. fat), 0 mg chol., 443 mg sodium, 26 g carb. (4 g fiber, 12 g sugars), 6 g pro. Exchanges: 2 vegetable, 0.5 starch, 0.5 carb., 3 fat.

Green Chile Chicken Tortilla Casserole

Enjoy all the flavors of tacos but with less mess. This casserole goes together just like a lasagna.

SERVINGS 8 ($^1/_8$ casserole each)
CARB. PER SERVING 24 g
PREP 45 minutes BROIL 6 minutes CHILL 8 hours BAKE 1 hour STAND 10 minutes

Nonstick cooking spray

1 pound tomatillos, outer husks removed, rinsed

1 teaspoon vegetable oil

1 fresh poblano chile pepper, seeded and chopped (see tip, *page 23*)

$^1/_2$ cup chopped onion (1 medium)

$^1/_4$ cup snipped fresh cilantro

1 teaspoon sugar*

$^1/_2$ teaspoon ground cumin

$^1/_4$ teaspoon salt

12 6-inch corn tortillas, halved

3 cups shredded cooked chicken breast

$1^3/_4$ cups shredded reduced-fat Mexican-style four-cheese blend (7 ounces)

1 16-ounce jar salsa

Chopped tomato, sliced fresh jalapeño chile peppers (see tip, *page 23*), and/or sliced green onions (optional)

PER SERVING: 280 cal., 9 g total fat (4 g sat. fat), 60 mg chol., 632 mg sodium, 24 g carb. (3 g fiber, 7 g sugars), 25 g pro. Exchanges: 2 vegetable, 1 starch, 2.5 lean meat, 1 fat.

PER SERVING WITH SUBSTITUTE: Same as above, except 279 cal.

1 Preheat broiler. Lightly coat a 2-quart square baking dish with cooking spray; set aside. Line a 15×10×1-inch baking pan with foil. Place tomatillos in the baking pan. Broil 4 to 5 inches from the heat for 6 to 8 minutes or until softened and charred, turning occasionally. Set aside to cool slightly.

2 In a large skillet heat oil over medium heat. Add poblano chile pepper and onion; cook and stir for 4 to 5 minutes or until tender and onion starts to brown.

3 In a blender or food processor combine tomatillos, onion mixture, the $^1/_4$ cup cilantro, the sugar, cumin, and salt. Cover and blend or process until smooth, stopping and scraping down sides as necessary.

4 Spread $^3/_4$ cup of the tomatillo mixture in the prepared baking dish. Arrange six of the tortilla halves over the sauce, overlapping slightly. Top with 1 cup of the chicken, $^1/_2$ cup of the cheese, and half of the salsa, spreading evenly. Add six more tortilla halves and top with 1 cup chicken, $^1/_2$ cup cheese, and half of the remaining tomatillo mixture, spreading evenly. Add six more tortilla halves, the remaining 1 cup chicken, and the remaining tomatillo mixture. Top with the remaining six tortilla halves and the remaining salsa, spreading to cover completely.

5 Cover dish with plastic wrap; chill for 8 to 24 hours. Cover and chill remaining $^3/_4$ cup cheese until needed.

6 Preheat oven to 375°F. Remove plastic wrap. Cover dish with foil. Bake for 40 minutes. Remove foil. Sprinkle with the remaining $^3/_4$ cup cheese. Bake about 20 minutes more or until heated through. Let stand for 10 minutes. If desired, top with chopped tomato, sliced jalapeños, and/or green onions.

*SUGAR SUBSTITUTE: Choose Splenda Sugar Blend for Baking. Follow package directions to use product amount equivalent to 1 teaspoon sugar.

QUICK TIP
Precooking and drying the zucchini slices prevent them from watering out as the lasagna bakes.

Zucchini and Turkey Lasagna

Here's a great way to use those zucchini that get away from you in the garden. They make a healthful, colorful stand-in for lasagna noodles.

SERVINGS 6 (^{1}/6 lasagna each)
CARB. PER SERVING 21 g
PREP 1 hour   COOK 21 minutes   BAKE 55 minutes at 350°F   STAND 20 minutes

8 ounces uncooked ground turkey breast

^{1}/4 cup finely chopped onion

2 tablespoons finely chopped red sweet pepper

2 tablespoons grated Parmesan cheese

2 tablespoons snipped fresh basil

^{1}/2 teaspoon dried Italian seasoning, crushed

^{1}/2 teaspoon crushed red pepper

1 tablespoon olive oil

^{1}/2 cup chopped onion (1 medium)

^{1}/2 cup shredded carrot (1 medium)

1 tablespoon bottled minced garlic (6 cloves)

1 teaspoon dried oregano, crushed

3 tablespoons tomato paste

1 28-ounce can crushed tomatoes, undrained

^{3}/4 cup fat-free cottage cheese

1 egg white

^{1}/8 teaspoon ground nutmeg

^{1}/4 cup shredded part-skim mozzarella cheese (1 ounce)

2 tablespoons snipped fresh basil

3 large zucchini

Nonstick cooking spray

2 tablespoons shredded part-skim mozzarella cheese

1 In a medium bowl combine ground turkey breast, the ^{1}/4 cup onion, the sweet pepper, Parmesan cheese, 2 tablespoons snipped basil, the Italian seasoning, and crushed red pepper; stir with a wooden spoon until well mixed. In a large skillet heat oil over medium heat. Add turkey mixture; cook until browned, using a wooden spoon to break up turkey mixture as it cooks. Using a slotted spoon, transfer turkey mixture to a large bowl; set aside.

2 In the same skillet cook the ^{1}/2 cup onion, the carrot, garlic, and oregano over medium heat about 5 minutes or until vegetables are softened. Stir in tomato paste; cook for 1 minute. Add crushed tomatoes. Bring to boiling; reduce heat. Simmer, uncovered, for 10 minutes. Set aside.

3 In a blender or small food processor combine cottage cheese, egg white, and nutmeg. Cover and blend or process until smooth. Stir in the ^{1}/4 cup mozzarella cheese and the basil. Set aside.

4 Cut zucchini lengthwise into ^{1}/4-inch-thick slices. Bring a large pot of water to boiling. Add zucchini slices; boil for 2 to 3 minutes or just until softened. Drain well. Pat zucchini slices dry with paper towels.

5 Preheat oven to 350°F. Lightly coat a 2-quart square baking dish with cooking spray. Spread ^{1}/2 cup of the tomato mixture in the bottom of the prepared baking dish. Top with a layer of the zucchini slices, overlapping slices slightly. Top with another ^{1}/2 cup of the tomato mixture, one-fourth of the turkey mixture, and ^{1}/4 cup of the cottage cheese mixture. Repeat layers three times. Top with the remaining tomato mixture.

6 Bake for 50 minutes to 1 hour or until heated through, draining off any excess liquid halfway through baking time. Sprinkle with 2 tablespoons mozzarella cheese. Bake about 5 minutes more or until cheese is melted. Let stand for 20 minutes before serving.

PER SERVING: 220 cal., 8 g total fat (2.33 g sat. fat), 33 mg chol., 468 mg sodium, 21 g carb. (5 g fiber, 13 g sugars), 18 g pro. Exchanges: 1 vegetable, 1 starch, 2 lean meat, 0.5 fat.

Bok Choy and Mango Stir-Fry with Skillet-Seared Barramundi

If you can't find baby bok choy, slice a mature bok choy head into strips for this stir-fry.

SERVINGS 4 (1 fish fillet, 1 cup vegetable mixture, and 1 tablespoon cashews each)
CARB. PER SERVING 17 g
PREP 30 minutes   MARINATE 1 hour
COOK 4 minutes

- 4 4-ounce fresh or frozen barramundi or tilapia fillets (with skin)
- 1 teaspoon finely shredded orange peel
- 1/3 cup orange juice
- 4 teaspoons reduced-sodium soy sauce
- 1 teaspoon grated fresh ginger
- 1/2 teaspoon toasted sesame oil
- 1/4 teaspoon salt
- 1/4 teaspoon black pepper
- 4 teaspoons vegetable oil
- 1 red sweet pepper, cut into bite-size strips
- 2 heads baby bok choy, trimmed and quartered (8 ounces)
- 1 medium mango, seeded, peeled, and cut into bite-size strips
- 1/4 cup coarsely chopped cashews

PER SERVING: 267 cal., 12 g total fat (2 g sat. fat), 46 mg chol., 499 mg sodium, 17 g carb. (2 g fiber, 12 g sugars), 24 g pro. Exchanges: 1 vegetable, 0.5 fruit, 3 lean meat, 2 fat.

1 | Thaw fish, if frozen. Rinse fish; pat dry with paper towels. Measure thickness of fish. Place fish in a large resealable plastic bag set in a shallow dish; set aside.

2 | For marinade, in a small bowl combine orange peel, orange juice, soy sauce, ginger, sesame oil, salt, and black pepper. Set aside half of the marinade. Pour the remaining marinade over fish in bag. Seal bag; turn to coat fish. Marinate in the refrigerator for 1 hour, turning bag occasionally. Chill the reserved marinade.

3 | Drain fish, discarding marinade. In a very large nonstick skillet heat 2 teaspoons of the vegetable oil over medium-high heat. Add fish, skin sides down. Cook for 4 to 6 minutes per 1/2-inch thickness of fish or until fish begins to flake when tested with a fork, turning once halfway through cooking time. Remove fish from skillet. Cover and keep warm.

4 | In the same skillet heat the remaining 2 teaspoons oil over medium-high heat. Add sweet pepper; cook and stir for 2 minutes. Add bok choy; cook and stir for 3 to 5 minutes more or just until vegetables are crisp-tender. Stir in mango and the reserved marinade. Heat through. Serve fish over vegetable mixture. Sprinkle with chopped cashews.

Pacific Northwest Paella

Salmon makes a robust and flavorful replacement for the seafood usually found in paella.

SERVINGS 6 (1$\frac{1}{2}$ cups each)
CARB. PER SERVING 32 g
START TO FINISH 45 minutes

- 1$\frac{1}{4}$ pounds fresh or frozen skinless salmon fillets, about 1 inch thick
- 4 slices applewood-smoked bacon
- 3 cups sliced fresh cremini or button mushrooms (8 ounces)
- 1 cup chopped onion (1 large)
- 2 cloves garlic, minced
- 2$\frac{1}{2}$ cups chicken broth
- 1 cup uncooked long grain white rice
- 2 teaspoons snipped fresh thyme or $\frac{1}{2}$ teaspoon dried thyme, crushed
- $\frac{1}{4}$ teaspoon cracked black pepper
- 1 pound fresh asparagus, trimmed and cut into 1-inch pieces, or one 10-ounce package frozen cut asparagus, thawed
- $\frac{1}{3}$ cup chopped roma tomato (1 medium)

PER SERVING: 313 cal., 9 g total fat (2 g sat. fat), 60 mg chol., 498 mg sodium, 32 g carb. (2 g fiber, 4 g sugars), 26 g pro. Exchanges: 1.5 vegetable, 1.5 starch, 2.5 lean meat, 1 fat.

1 Thaw fish, if frozen. Meanwhile, in a large deep skillet or paella pan cook bacon over medium heat until crisp. Drain bacon on paper towels, reserving drippings in skillet. Crumble bacon; set aside.

2 Add mushrooms, onion, and garlic to the reserved drippings in skillet. Cook about 5 minutes or until onion is tender, stirring occasionally. Stir in broth, rice, and thyme. Bring to boiling; reduce heat. Simmer, covered, for 10 minutes.

3 Meanwhile, rinse fish; pat dry with paper towels. Cut fish into 1-inch pieces. Sprinkle with pepper; toss gently.

4 Place fish and asparagus on top of rice mixture. Simmer, covered, for 10 to 12 minutes or until fish flakes easily when tested with a fork and asparagus is crisp-tender. Sprinkle with tomato and crumbled bacon.

Chia-Crusted Tuna with Mango Salsa

Chia seeds give tuna a nutty crunch while passing on healthful fiber and omega-3 fatty acids. Bonus: Almost all of chia's carbs are from fiber.

SERVINGS 2 (1 tuna fillet and $^1/_3$ cup salsa each)
CARB. PER SERVING 18 g
PREP 30 minutes   COOK 10 minutes   ROAST 10 minutes at 425°F   STAND 2 minutes

¼ cup coarsely chopped fresh mango*

¼ cup coarsely chopped fresh pineapple*

2 fresh strawberries, diced

1 tablespoon snipped fresh cilantro

1 teaspoon lime juice

¼ cup packed brown sugar**

¼ cup balsamic vinegar

¼ cup water

2 5- to 6-ounce fresh or frozen tuna fillets

⅛ teaspoon coarsely ground black pepper

1 tablespoon whole chia seeds

1 teaspoon canola oil

PER SERVING: 263 cal., 5 g total fat (1 g sat. fat), 55 mg chol., 69 mg sodium, 18 g carb. (3 g fiber, 13 g sugars), 36 g pro. Exchanges: 0.5 fruit, 0.5 carb., 5 lean meat.

1 For salsa, in a medium bowl combine mango and pineapple. Add strawberries, cilantro, and lime juice. Toss to combine. Set aside.

2 For glaze, in a small nonstick saucepan combine brown sugar, balsamic vinegar, and the water. Bring to boiling; reduce heat. Simmer, uncovered, for 10 to 12 minutes or until mixture reaches the consistency of maple syrup and coats the back of a metal spoon, stirring frequently. Let stand to cool completely (mixture will thicken as it cools).***

3 Thaw tuna, if frozen. Preheat oven to 425°F. Rinse fish; pat dry with paper towels. Sprinkle tuna with the pepper. Spread chia seeds on a plate. Press each tuna fillet into the chia seeds to evenly coat one side.

4 Coat a shallow nonstick or foil-lined baking pan with the oil. Place tuna, chia seed sides up, in prepared baking pan. Roast for 10 to 12 minutes or until tuna is firm to the touch and an instant-read thermometer inserted in centers registers 145°F (centers may still be pink); do not turn tuna over during roasting. Remove tuna from the oven; let stand for 2 to 3 minutes before serving.

5 To serve, drizzle each plate with 1 to 2 teaspoons of the glaze (store any remaining glaze in the refrigerator for another use); top with cooked tuna. Spoon salsa over tuna.

*TEST KITCHEN TIP: If fresh mango and/or pineapple is not available, use canned or jarred fruit instead.

**SUGAR SUBSTITUTES: We do not recommend using a sugar substitute for this recipe.

***TEST KITCHEN TIP: The glaze can be made ahead and stored in the refrigerator for up to 1 month.

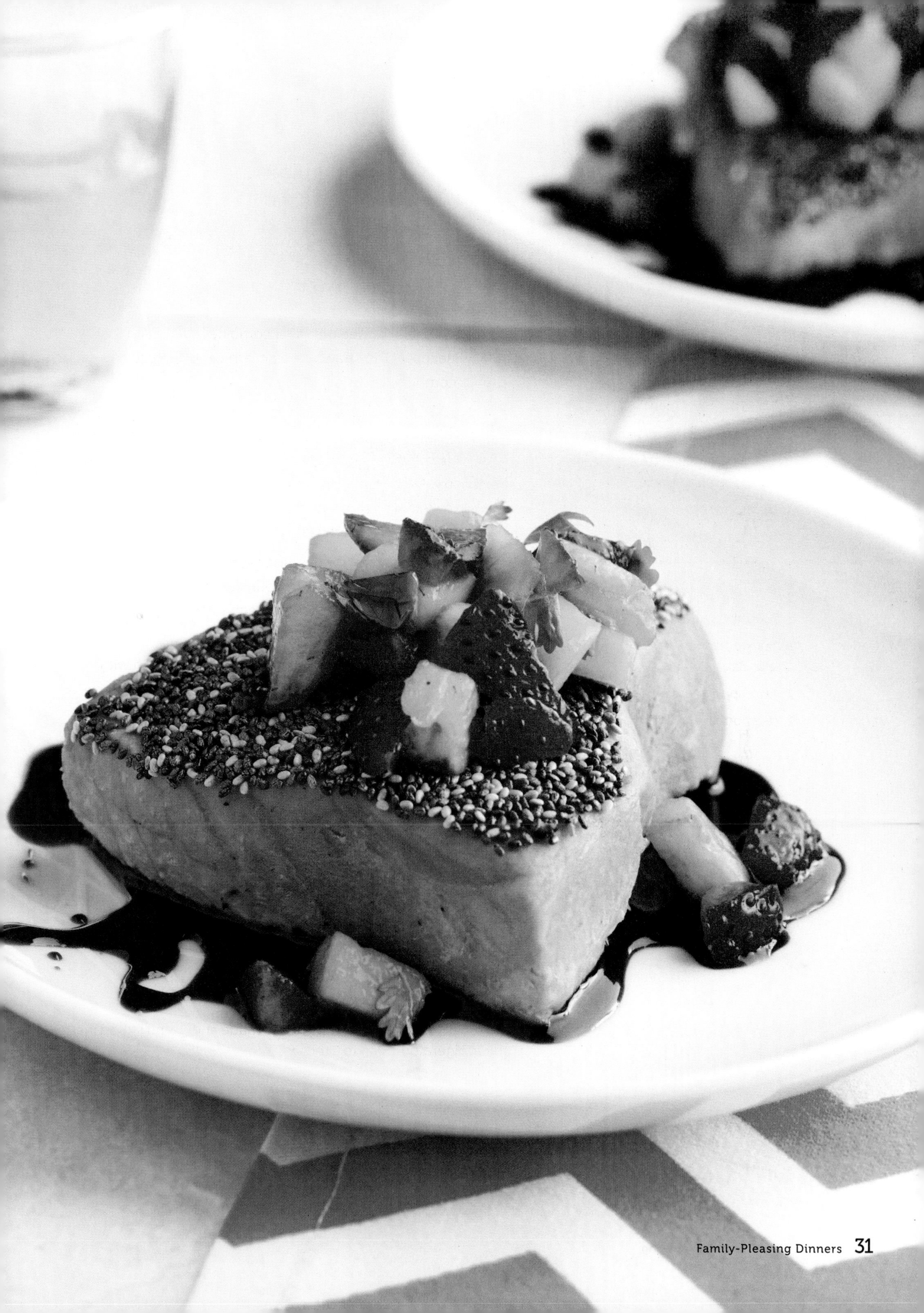

Fish Tostadas with Chili-Lime Cream

Use coleslaw mix as an alternative to chopped iceberg lettuce for a healthful tostada topping that also saves time.

》 SERVINGS 4 (2 tostadas each)
CARB. PER SERVING 22 g
START TO FINISH 20 minutes

1 pound fresh or frozen tilapia or cod fillets

1/2 teaspoon chili powder

1/4 teaspoon salt

1 lime, halved

1/2 cup light sour cream

1/2 teaspoon garlic powder

8 6-inch tostada shells

2 cups packaged shredded cabbage with carrot (coleslaw mix)

1 avocado, halved, seeded, peeled, and sliced (optional)

1 cup cherry tomatoes, quartered

Bottled hot pepper sauce (optional)

PER SERVING: 282 cal., 11 g total fat (3 g sat. fat), 65 mg chol., 408 mg sodium, 22 g carb. (3 g fiber, 2 g sugars), 26 g pro. Exchanges: 1 vegetable, 1 starch, 3 lean meat, 1 fat.

1 Thaw fish, if frozen. Rinse fish; pat dry with paper towels. Sprinkle fish with 1/4 teaspoon of the chili powder and the salt; set aside. Preheat broiler.

2 For chili-lime cream, in a small bowl squeeze 2 teaspoons juice from half of the lime. Stir in sour cream, garlic powder, and the remaining 1/4 teaspoon chili powder; set aside. Cut the remaining lime half into wedges; set aside.

3 Place fish on the unheated greased rack of a broiler pan; tuck under thin edges to make fish an even thickness. Measure thickness of fish. Place tostada shells on a baking sheet. Place in oven on the lowest rack. Broil fish 4 to 5 inches from heat for 4 to 6 minutes per 1/2-inch thickness or until fish flakes easily when tested with a fork. Break fish into chunks. Top tostada shells with fish, coleslaw mix, avocado (if desired), tomatoes, hot pepper sauce (if desired), and chili-lime cream. Serve with the reserved lime wedges.

Almond-Thyme-Crusted Mahi Mahi

Almonds give the coating on this fish flavor, crunch, and healthful fats. Using egg whites to hold the coating in place helps keep fat in check.

SERVINGS 4 (1 fish fillet each)
CARB. PER SERVING 6 g
PREP 25 minutes
BAKE 4 minutes at 450°F

Nonstick cooking spray

4 4- to 5-ounce fresh or frozen mahi mahi fillets

1 egg white, lightly beaten

1 tablespoon water

$\frac{1}{3}$ cup sliced almonds, coarsely broken

2 tablespoons fine dry bread crumbs

1 tablespoon snipped fresh thyme

$\frac{1}{4}$ teaspoon salt

1 tablespoon light butter with canola oil

1 tablespoon finely chopped shallot

$1\frac{1}{2}$ teaspoons flour

$\frac{1}{8}$ teaspoon salt

Dash black pepper

$\frac{1}{2}$ cup Chardonnay or other dry white wine

1 tablespoon lemon juice

$\frac{1}{2}$ teaspoon snipped fresh thyme

Snipped fresh thyme (optional)

PER SERVING: 203 cal., 6 g total fat (1 g sat. fat), 84 mg chol., 383 mg sodium, 6 g carb. (1 g fiber, 1 g sugars), 24 g pro. Exchanges: 0.5 starch, 3 lean meat, 1 fat.

1 | Preheat oven to 450°F. Line a baking sheet with foil. Coat foil with cooking spray; set aside. Thaw fish, if frozen. Rinse fish; pat dry with paper towels. Measure thickness of fish; set aside.

2 | In a shallow dish combine egg white and the water. In another shallow dish combine almonds, bread crumbs, the 1 tablespoon thyme, and the $\frac{1}{4}$ teaspoon salt. Dip fillets in egg white mixture, turning to coat. Dip in almond mixture, turning to evenly coat fish.

3 | Place fish on prepared baking sheet. Sprinkle any remaining almond mixture over fish. Coat fish with cooking spray. Bake for 4 to 6 minutes per $\frac{1}{2}$-inch thickness or until fish begins to flake easily when tested with a fork.

4 | Meanwhile, in a small saucepan melt butter over medium heat. Add shallot; cook for 3 minutes, stirring occasionally. Add flour, the $\frac{1}{8}$ teaspoon salt, and the pepper, stirring until flour is coated. Add white wine and lemon juice all at once. Cook and stir until thickened and bubbly. Cook and stir for 1 minute more. Remove from heat. Stir in the $\frac{1}{2}$ teaspoon thyme. To serve, drizzle sauce over fish. If desired, garnish with additional snipped thyme.

QUICK TIP
To cut prep time, use
precooked jasmine rice,
such as Uncle Ben's Ready
Rice brand.

Vegetarian Fried Rice

Bump up the veggies in fried rice and add some tofu to make this
Asian side dish a featured player at dinner.

SERVINGS 6 (1^1/3 cups each)
CARB. PER SERVING 30 g
PREP 30 minutes MARINATE 30 minutes COOK 20 minutes

8   ounces organic extra-firm tofu
    (fresh bean curd)

1   tablespoon Asian chili sauce
    (Sriracha sauce)

6   teaspoons olive oil

^{1}/2 teaspoon grated fresh ginger

1^1/2 cups frozen shelled sweet soybeans
    (edamame)

1   cup thinly sliced carrots (2 medium)

1   pound fresh asparagus spears,
    trimmed and cut into 2-inch-long
    pieces (2 cups)

1   cup frozen snow pea pods

1   cup refrigerated or frozen egg
    product, thawed

2   teaspoons toasted sesame oil

2   cups cooked jasmine rice

1   8-ounce can sliced water
    chestnuts, drained, rinsed,
    and chopped

2   tablespoons reduced-sodium
    soy sauce

1   tablespoon sesame seeds, toasted

PER SERVING: 283 cal., 12 g total fat
(2 g sat. fat), 19 mg chol.,
318 mg sodium, 30 g carb. (4 g fiber,
5 g sugars), 15 g pro. Exchanges:
1 vegetable, 1.5 starch, 1.5 lean
meat, 1.5 fat.

1 Drain tofu well. Cut tofu into ^{1}/2- to ^{3}/4-inch cubes. In a
small bowl combine tofu and chili sauce; gently stir to
coat. Marinate at room temperature for 30 minutes or in the
refrigerator for up to 4 hours.

2 Meanwhile, in a very large nonstick skillet or wok heat
2 teaspoons of the olive oil over medium-high heat.
Add ginger; cook for 30 seconds. Add frozen edamame and
carrots; stir-fry for 3 minutes. Add asparagus and frozen pea
pods; stir-fry about 5 minutes more or until crisp-tender but
still brightly colored. Quickly transfer vegetables to a large
bowl; cover to keep warm.

3 Add 2 teaspoons of the remaining olive oil to the
hot skillet. Add marinated tofu to hot oil; fry for 5 to
7 minutes or until crisp on all sides, turning to crisp evenly.
Transfer tofu to bowl with the vegetables.

4 Add the remaining 2 teaspoons olive oil to the skillet.
When oil is heated, pour in egg. Cook over medium
heat, without stirring, until mixture begins to set on the
bottom and around the edges. Using a metal spatula, lift edges
of the cooked egg, allowing the uncooked portion to flow
underneath. Continue to cook for 2 to 3 minutes or until egg is
cooked through but still glossy and moist. Remove from heat.
Using the spatula, chop egg into bite-size chunks; transfer to
the large bowl with vegetables.

5 Add the toasted sesame oil to the skillet; heat over
medium-high heat. Add the cooked rice. Using a spatula
or spoon, break up any chunks; cook rice until grains are
coated with oil. Add cooked vegetables, tofu, and egg. Add
water chestnuts and soy sauce; stir gently to combine. Heat
through. Sprinkle with sesame seeds. Serve immediately.

Macaroni Pancakes with Mushrooms, Spinach, and Tomatoes

Yes, you can do that with macaroni! This layered dish will add a surprise to dinner.

SERVINGS 6 (1 wedge each)
CARB. PER SERVING 22 g
PREP 1 hour **BAKE** 5 minutes at 375°F
STAND 10 minutes

- 3 ounces dried whole wheat elbow macaroni
- 2 cloves garlic, thinly sliced
- 5 teaspoons olive oil
- 1 14.5-ounce can no-salt-added diced tomatoes, undrained
- ¾ teaspoon kosher salt
- ½ teaspoon black pepper
- ½ teaspoon dried Italian seasoning, crushed
- 10 ounces fresh cremini mushrooms, sliced
- 1 10-ounce package frozen chopped spinach, thawed and well drained
- 6 eggs
- 1½ cups finely shredded carrots (2 to 3 medium)
- 1 cup shredded reduced-fat mozzarella cheese (4 ounces)

Snipped fresh oregano (optional)

PER SERVING: 259 cal., 12 g total fat (3 g sat. fat), 193 mg chol., 536 mg sodium, 22 g carb. (5 g fiber, 5 g sugars), 17 g pro. Exchanges: 1 vegetable, 1 starch, 2 medium-fat meat, 1 fat.

1 Cook macaroni according to package directions. Drain; set aside.

2 In a large skillet cook garlic in 1 teaspoon of the oil for 30 seconds. Add tomatoes, a pinch of the salt, a pinch of the pepper, and ¼ teaspoon of the Italian seasoning. Bring to boiling; reduce heat. Simmer, uncovered, for 5 to 8 minutes until most of the liquid is gone. Transfer to a bowl; set aside.

3 In the same skillet cook mushrooms in another 1 teaspoon of the oil about 5 minutes or until liquid is evaporated. Stir in thawed spinach, another pinch of the salt, another pinch of the pepper, and the remaining ¼ teaspoon Italian seasoning. Cook and stir until most of the liquid from the spinach is evaporated; set aside.

4 Preheat oven to 375°F. In a medium bowl whisk two of the eggs until combined. Stir in one-third of the shredded carrots and one-third of the cooked macaroni. Season with another pinch of the salt and another pinch of the pepper. In a nonstick skillet heat another 1 teaspoon of the oil over medium-low heat. Add macaroni mixture; cook until macaroni mixture is set and lightly browned on one side. Remove from heat. Place a plate over the skillet; holding plate and skillet firmly, invert pancake onto the plate. Slide pancake back into the skillet. Cook until lightly browned; slide onto a greased cookie sheet and keep warm. Repeat two more times to make three pancakes total.

5 Place one of the pancakes in a greased 9-inch pie plate. Spread mushroom-spinach mixture to within ½ inch of the edge of the pancake. Sprinkle with ¼ cup of the shredded cheese. Top with a second pancake; spread tomato mixture over pancake to within ½ inch of the edge of the pancake. Sprinkle with ¼ cup of the shredded cheese. Top with the final pancake; sprinkle with the remaining ½ cup shredded cheese.

6 Bake for 5 to 8 minutes or until hot in center and cheese is melted. Let stand for 10 minutes before serving. If desired, garnish with snipped oregano. To serve, cut stacked pancakes into six wedges.

Penne with Five Herbs

Raid the herb garden for all kinds of flavor in this simple pasta toss. If you can't find ricotta salata, feta or queso fresco makes a good substitute.

SERVINGS 6 ($1^{1}/_{2}$ cups each)
CARB. PER SERVING 33 g
PREP 20 minutes COOK 13 minutes

- 8 ounces dried penne pasta
- 2 tablespoons extra virgin olive oil
- $^{1}/_{3}$ cup snipped fresh basil
- 1 teaspoon snipped fresh oregano
- 1 teaspoon fresh thyme leaves
- $^{1}/_{2}$ teaspoon cracked black pepper
- 4 cups grape tomatoes
- 2 cloves garlic, minced
- $^{1}/_{2}$ cup vegetable broth
- $^{1}/_{4}$ cup snipped fresh Italian (flat-leaf) parsley
- 2 tablespoons snipped fresh chives
- $1^{1}/_{2}$ cups crumbled ricotta salata

1 Cook pasta according to package directions; drain well. Transfer drained pasta to a large bowl. Add 1 tablespoon of the oil, the basil, oregano, thyme, and pepper. Toss to combine; cover to keep warm.

2 In a very large skillet heat the remaining 1 tablespoon oil over medium-high heat. Add tomatoes and garlic; cook and stir for 5 to 6 minutes or until tomatoes caramelize, skins burst, and tomatoes begin to break down. Stir in broth; bring to boiling.

3 Add tomato mixture, parsley, and chives to pasta mixture; gently toss to combine. Divide pasta mixture among six serving plates. Top with ricotta salata.

PER SERVING: 285 cal., 11 g total fat (1 g sat. fat), 25 mg chol., 556 mg sodium, 33 g carb. (3 g fiber, 4 g sugars), 11 g pro. Exchanges: 0.5 vegetable, 2 starch, 0.5 high-fat meat, 1 fat.

Grilled Tofu with Fennel Chutney

Use a food processor to evenly slice the onions and fennel. If you prefer to use a knife, be careful and cut the vegetables into even slices.

>> SERVINGS 8 (1 tofu portion, 2 tomatoes, and 3 tablespoons chutney each)
CARB. PER SERVING 17 g
PREP 30 minutes CHILL 1 hour MARINATE 1 hour COOK 26 minutes

2 14-ounce packages extra-firm tofu (fresh bean curd), drained

1½ cups fresh basil leaves

⅓ cup water

3 tablespoons olive oil

4 cloves garlic

2 teaspoons balsamic vinegar

1 teaspoon kosher salt

½ teaspoon freshly ground black pepper

2 tablespoons olive oil

3 medium onions, thinly sliced

1 bulb fennel, cored and thinly sliced

½ cup thinly sliced fresh basil

¼ cup pine nuts, toasted

¼ cup dried currants

1 tablespoon balsamic vinegar

½ teaspoon kosher salt

¼ teaspoon freshly ground black pepper

4 large beefsteak-style tomatoes

½ teaspoon kosher salt

¼ teaspoon freshly ground black pepper

Nonstick cooking spray

PER SERVING: 255 cal., 18 g total fat (2 g sat. fat), 0 mg chol., 523 mg sodium, 17 g carb. (4 g fiber, 8 g sugars), 13 g pro. Exchanges: 2 vegetable, 0.5 fruit, 2 medium-fat meat, 2 fat.

1 | Line a 15×10×1-inch baking pan with paper towels. Place drained tofu on the paper towels; top with additional paper towels and then top with a baking sheet. Place two or three cans of food on the baking sheet to weight it down. Chill about 1 hour or until each block of tofu is reduced in thickness by a third. Slice one block of the pressed tofu vertically in half and then horizontally so you have four pieces, each about the size of a deck of cards. Repeat with the remaining tofu block to make eight pieces total.

2 | In a food processor combine the 1½ cups basil, the water, the 3 tablespoons olive oil, the garlic, the 2 teaspoons balsamic vinegar, the 1 teaspoon kosher salt, and the ½ teaspoon pepper. Cover and process until smooth. Set aside ¼ cup of the mixture.

3 | Place tofu pieces in a resealable plastic bag set in a shallow dish. Add the remaining basil mixture. Seal bag; turn to coat tofu. Marinate in the refrigerator for 1 hour.

4 | Meanwhile, for chutney, in a large skillet heat the 2 tablespoons olive oil over medium-low heat. Add onions and fennel; cook 20 minutes or until golden brown, stirring occasionally. Remove from heat. Stir in the ½ cup basil, the pine nuts, currants, the 1 tablespoon balsamic vinegar, ½ teaspoon salt, and ¼ teaspoon pepper. Set aside.

5 | Core and slice tomatoes into ½- to ¾-inch-thick slices (about 16 slices). Pat tomato slices dry with paper towels. Season with ½ teaspoon kosher salt and ¼ teaspoon pepper. Remove tofu pieces from marinade; discard marinade. Pat tofu dry with paper towels.

6 | Coat a grill pan with cooking spray. Heat pan over high heat. Place tomato slices on grill pan; cook 2 minutes, turning once and changing the direction slices are placed on the grill pan halfway through the cooking of each side. Transfer tomato slices to a platter. Cook tofu slices on hot grill pan for 4 minutes, turning as directed for the tomatoes. Cook tomatoes and tofu in batches if necessary; coat pan with cooking spray as needed. Serve tomatoes and tofu with the chutney. Drizzle tomatoes with the reserved basil mixture.

QUICK TIP
Make sure to use extra-firm tofu.
It needs to remain in solid portions
when sliced and grilled.

fresh
salad meals

Whether cold or hot, tossed or arranged, salads are some of

most nutritionally packed and visually appealing meals. With

ingredients ranging from leafy greens and vibrant vegetables to

succulent meats and toothsome pasta, this recipe assortment

promises pure dining pleasure.

Flank Steak and Plum Salad with Creamy Chimichurri Dressing

Plums range in color from deep purple and rosy red to apple green and peachy gold. Choose plums that are ripe and ready to eat.

SERVINGS 4 (1½ ounces cooked meat, about 2 cups salad, and about 2 tablespoons dressing each)
CARB. PER SERVING 14 g
PREP 20 minutes GRILL 10 minutes STAND 5 minutes

- 8   ounces beef flank steak
- 1   teaspoon ground cumin
- ¼   teaspoon salt
- 1   medium red onion, cut into ½-inch-thick slices
- 2   teaspoons olive oil
- ¼   teaspoon freshly ground black pepper
- 6   cups mâche (lamb's lettuce) or baby greens
- 4   firm yet ripe plums, pitted and cut into wedges
- 1   recipe Creamy Chimichurri Dressing

1 Trim fat from meat. Sprinkle both sides of meat with cumin and the salt. Brush onion slices on all sides with oil; sprinkle with pepper. For a charcoal or gas grill, grill meat and onion slices on the rack of a covered grill directly over medium-hot heat for 10 to 14 minutes for medium rare to medium (145°F to 160°F); grill onion slices about 10 minutes or until tender, turning both meat and onion slices once halfway through grilling time. Remove meat and onion slices from grill. Let meat stand for 5 minutes. Thinly slice meat.

2 Place mâche in a large salad bowl or arrange on a large platter. Top with meat, onion, and plum wedges. Serve with half of the Creamy Chimichurri Dressing. (Save other half of the dressing for another use.)

CREAMY CHIMICHURRI DRESSING: In a small bowl stir together ¾ cup light mayonnaise; ¼ cup plain fat-free Greek yogurt or sour cream; 1 tablespoon white vinegar; and 3 cloves garlic, minced. Stir in 3 tablespoons snipped fresh Italian (flat-leaf) parsley, ½ teaspoon crushed red pepper, and ⅛ teaspoon salt. Serve immediately or cover and refrigerate for up to 1 week. Before serving, if necessary, stir in enough milk to reach desired consistency.

14 grams carb.

PER SERVING: 231 cal., 13 g total fat (3 g sat. fat), 42 mg chol., 371 mg sodium, 14 g carb. (2 g fiber, 9 g sugars), 15 g pro. Exchanges: 0.5 fruit, 0.5 starch, 2 lean meat, 2 fat.

Very Berry Grilled Pork Salad

The blackberry-raspberry combo gives the dressing an intense color. If you opt to use only one type of berry, expect a different dressing color.

SERVINGS 6 (1½ cups salad, 3 ounces pork, and about 3 tablespoons dressing each)
CARB. PER SERVING 11 g
PREP 25 minutes STAND 1 hour GRILL 25 minutes

½ of a medium red onion, cut into very thin wedges
⅓ cup red wine vinegar
2 12-ounce pork tenderloins
½ teaspoon salt
½ teaspoon black pepper
1½ cups fresh blackberries*
1½ cups fresh raspberries*
¼ cup snipped fresh basil
2 tablespoons olive oil
⅛ teaspoon salt
9 cups fresh baby spinach
½ cup very thinly sliced celery (1 stalk)
4 ounces semisoft goat cheese (chèvre), crumbled

1 | In a small bowl combine red onion and vinegar. Cover and let stand at room temperature for 1 hour or chill up to 24 hours, stirring occasionally.

2 | Trim fat from pork. Sprinkle pork with the ½ teaspoon salt and the pepper. For a charcoal grill, arrange hot coals around a drip pan. Test for medium-hot heat above drip pan. Place pork on grill rack over the drip pan. Cover and grill for 25 to 30 minutes or until an instant-read thermometer inserted into the center of the pork registers 145°F. (For a gas grill, preheat grill. Reduce heat to medium-high. Adjust for indirect cooking. Place meat on grill rack over burner that is off. Grill as directed.) Transfer pork to a cutting board. Cover with foil; let stand for 3 minutes.

3 | Meanwhile, place ½ cup of the blackberries and ½ cup of the raspberries in a blender or food processor. Cover and blend or process until smooth. Press pureed berries through a fine-mesh sieve; discard seeds. In a small bowl stir together strained berries, basil, oil, and the ⅛ teaspoon salt. Set aside.

4 | To serve, divide spinach among six serving plates. Using a fork, remove onion from vinegar, allowing excess vinegar to drip off; reserve vinegar. Arrange onion on spinach on plates; top with celery. Thinly slice pork crosswise; place on top of salads.

5 | For dressing, stir the reserved vinegar into the pureed berry mixture. Drizzle dressing over salads. Top salads with the remaining fresh berries and the goat cheese.

*TEST KITCHEN TIP: If desired, substute 3 cups fresh boysenberries for the blackberries and raspberries. Puree 1 cup of the boysenberries until smooth; press through a sieve and discard seeds. Top salads with remaining 2 cups berries.

PER SERVING: 282 cal., 13 g total fat (5 g sat. fat), 88 mg chol., 431 mg sodium, 11 g carb. (5 g fiber, 6 g sugars), 30 g pro.
Exchanges: 1 vegetable, 0.5 fruit, 4 lean meat, 1 fat.

Chicken and Artichoke Salad

Store the leftover artichoke hearts in an airtight container in the refrigerator for 3 days and toss into your next salad or stir into pasta sauce.

SERVINGS 4 ($^{1}/_{2}$ cup salad and 4 bagel crisps each)
CARB. PER SERVING 20 g
START TO FINISH 15 minutes

- 8 ounces cooked chicken breast, chopped
- $^{2}/_{3}$ cup canned artichoke hearts, rinsed, drained, and chopped
- $^{1}/_{4}$ cup packaged shredded carrots
- $^{1}/_{4}$ cup spinach-artichoke Greek yogurt veggie dip, such as Marzetti Otria brand
- $^{1}/_{4}$ cup fat-free mayonnaise dressing or salad dressing
- $^{1}/_{4}$ teaspoon salt
- $^{1}/_{4}$ teaspoon black pepper
- 4 cups packaged fresh baby spinach
- 4 teaspoons pine nuts, toasted
- 16 plain bagel crisps, such as New-York-style brand

PER SERVING: 237 cal., 7 g total fat (3 g sat. fat), 44 mg chol., 581 mg sodium, 20 g carb. (3 g fiber, 3 g sugars), 18 g pro. Exchanges: 1 vegetable, 1 starch, 2 lean meat, 1 fat.

1 | In a medium bowl combine chicken, artichokes, carrots, spinach-artichoke dip, mayonnaise dressing, salt, and pepper.

2 | To serve, divide spinach among four serving plates. Spoon chicken mixture on top of spinach. Sprinkle with pine nuts. Serve with bagel crisps.

QUICK TIP
Serve the leftover spinach-artichoke Greek yogurt veggie dip with assorted veggies for a healthful snack.

Red-on-Red Chicken Salad with Honey-Balsamic Drizzle

Decide how fussy you want to be with the watermelon—simply cut it into chunks or use a melon baller to carefully scoop into bite-size balls.

SERVINGS 4 (2^1/$_2$ cups each)
CARB. PER SERVING 32 g
PREP 30 minutes CHILL 45 minutes

- ^{1}/$_2$ cup balsamic vinegar
- 2 tablespoons honey
- 1 2^1/$_2$- to 3^1/$_2$-pound seedless baby watermelon
- 2 cups quartered fresh strawberries
- 2 cups chopped roasted chicken breast (10 ounces)
- ^{1}/$_2$ of a small red onion, halved and very thinly sliced
- ^{1}/$_2$ cup fresh basil leaves, cut into thin strips
- ^{1}/$_2$ cup crumbled feta cheese (2 ounces)

  Chopped pecans, toasted (optional)

PER SERVING: 285 cal., 7 g total fat (3 g sat. fat), 80 mg chol., 461 mg sodium, 32 g carb. (2 g fiber, 27 g sugars), 25 g pro. Exchanges: 1 fruit, 1 carb., 3.5 lean meat, 0.5 fat.

PER SERVING SPINACH SALAD: Same as above, except 294 cal., 488 mg sodium, 34 g carb. (3 g fiber), 26 g pro. Exchanges: 0.5 vegetable.

1 For drizzle, in a small saucepan combine vinegar and honey. Bring to boiling over medium-high heat; reduce heat. Simmer for 7 to 8 minutes or until mixture is reduced by half, stirring frequently. Cool.

2 Cut watermelon crosswise into 1-inch slices; remove the flesh from slices. (If desired, reserve rind from four of the slices to use as salad bowl rings.) Cut watermelon flesh into ^{1}/$_2$-inch cubes (or use a small melon baller to make ^{3}/$_4$-inch balls) and place in a very large bowl. Add strawberries, chicken, red onion, basil, and cheese; mix very gently. Cover and chill about 45 minutes or until cold.

3 To serve, if using, place the four watermelon rings on chilled salad plates. Divide the chicken mixture among chilled salad plates. Drizzle each serving with 1 tablespoon of the vinegar mixture. If desired, sprinkle with pecans.

RED-ON-RED CHICKEN AND SPINACH SALAD: Omit the watermelon salad bowl rings. Divide one 5-ounce package fresh baby spinach among four chilled salad plates. Spoon the chicken mixture on top of spinach. Drizzle each serving with 1 tablespoon of the vinegar mixture and, if desired, sprinkle with pecans.

Chicken, Spinach, and Pasta Salad

For a salad with more Italian flair and a spicier bite, use a bag of baby arugula in place of the spinach.

SERVINGS 6 (1²/₃ cups each)
CARB. PER SERVING 26 g
START TO FINISH 30 minutes

- 6 ounces dried multigrain penne pasta
- Nonstick cooking spray
- 8 ounces skinless, boneless chicken breast halves, cut into 1-inch pieces
- 1 cup sliced fresh mushrooms
- ¼ cup chopped onion
- 1 clove garlic, minced
- 3 tablespoons olive oil
- 3 tablespoons balsamic vinegar
- 3 tablespoons snipped fresh basil or 2 teaspoons dried basil, crushed
- ¼ teaspoon salt
- ⅛ teaspoon black pepper
- 1 6-ounce package fresh baby spinach or spinach
- 1 cup seeded and chopped roma tomatoes (3 medium)
- ¼ cup shredded Parmesan cheese (1 ounce)

1 | Cook pasta according to package directions; drain. Rinse with cold water; drain again. Meanwhile, coat a large nonstick skillet with cooking spray; heat skillet over medium heat. Add chicken, mushrooms, onion, and garlic; cook for 8 to 10 minutes or until chicken is no longer pink and vegetables are tender, stirring occasionally. Cool slightly.

2 | In a very large bowl combine cooked pasta and chicken mixture. For vinaigrette, in a small screw-top jar combine oil, vinegar, basil, salt, and pepper. Cover and shake well.

3 | Pour vinaigrette over pasta mixture; toss gently to coat. Add spinach, tomatoes, and cheese; toss gently to combine.

10 grams fat

PER SERVING: 250 cal., 10 g total fat (2 g sat. fat), 28 mg chol., 239 mg sodium, 26 g carb. (4 g fiber, 4 g sugars), 15 g pro. Exchanges: 0.5 vegetable, 1.5 starch, 1.5 lean meat, 1 fat.

Nectarine, Beet, and Goat Cheese Salad

Packaged cooked whole baby beets are a great go-to, but if you have beets growing in your garden, cook your own.

SERVINGS 4 (1 cup spinach plus toppings each)
CARB. PER SERVING 22 g
START TO FINISH 20 minutes

- 4 cups fresh baby spinach leaves
- 2 8-ounce packages refrigerated cooked whole baby beets, quartered
- 1 cup shredded cooked chicken (5 ounces)
- 2 fresh nectarines, pitted and cut into wedges
- 2 ounces crumbled soft goat cheese
- ¼ cup bottled balsamic vinaigrette salad dressing
- ¼ teaspoon salt
- ⅛ teaspoon black pepper

1 | Divide spinach among four large salad plates or bowls. Top with beets, chicken, nectarines, and goat cheese. Drizzle 1 tablespoon vinaigrette on each salad. Season with the salt and pepper.

PER SERVING: 238 cal., 10 g total fat (3 g sat. fat), 38 mg chol., 480 mg sodium, 22 g carb. (5 g fiber, 17 g sugars), 16 g pro. Exchanges: 3 vegetable, 0.5 fruit, 1.5 lean meat, 1.5 fat.

Turkey Salad with Oranges

Several orange varieties fall within the "navel" category. For a bright flavor and color, try Cara Cara oranges.

SERVINGS 4 (2 cups salad and 2 tablespoons dressing each)
CARB. PER SERVING 25 g
START TO FINISH 30 minutes

- 1   5-ounce package arugula or baby spinach
- 12   ounces cooked turkey or chicken, shredded
- 1   red sweet pepper, cut into strips (1 cup)
- ¼   cup fresh cilantro
- 3   tablespoons orange juice
- 2   tablespoons peanut oil or canola oil
- 1   tablespoon honey
- 2   teaspoons lemon juice
- 2   teaspoons Dijon-style mustard
- ¼   teaspoon ground cumin
- ¼   teaspoon salt
- ¼   teaspoon black pepper
- 4   oranges, peeled and sectioned

1 In a large bowl toss together arugula, turkey, sweet pepper, and cilantro.

2 For vinaigrette, in a small bowl whisk together orange juice, oil, honey, lemon juice, mustard, cumin, salt, and black pepper. Drizzle vinaigrette over salad; toss gently to coat. To serve, add orange sections to salad.

PER SERVING: 281 cal., 8 g total fat (1 g sat. fat), 71 mg chol., 263 mg sodium, 25 g carb. (5 g fiber, 20 g sugars), 28 g pro. Exchanges: 1.5 vegetable, 1 fruit, 3.5 lean meat, 0.5 fat.

Lobster Roll Salad with Bacon Vinaigrette

If you love crab, swap cooked crabmeat for the lobster. Because crab legs are almost always precooked, you can skip grilling and simply remove the meat from the legs.

SERVINGS 6 (2 cups each)
CARB. PER SERVING 22 g
PREP 35 minutes GRILL 25 minutes

- 2 8-ounce fresh or frozen spiny lobster tails
- 2 tablespoons olive oil
- 2 cloves garlic, minced
- 6 ounces whole grain ciabatta rolls, halved horizontally
- 6 slices lower-sodium and less-fat bacon, such as Farmland brand
- 3 tablespoons white wine vinegar
- 2 tablespoons finely chopped shallot
- 2 tablespoons finely snipped fresh chives
- 1 tablespoon olive oil
- 2 cups fresh baby spinach
- 2 cups torn romaine lettuce
- 3 medium tomatoes, cut into wedges (about 1$\frac{1}{2}$ cups)
- 1 cup coarsely chopped, seeded cucumber
- 1 cup coarsely chopped red sweet peppers (2 small)

PER SERVING: 277 cal., 12 g total fat (2 g sat. fat), 48 mg chol., 360 mg sodium, 22 g carb. (3 g fiber, 3 g sugars), 18 g pro. Exchanges: 1 vegetable, 1 starch, 2 lean meat, 2 fat.

1 Thaw lobster tails, if frozen. Rinse tails; pat dry with paper towels. To butterfly lobster tails, use kitchen shears or a sharp heavy knife to cut lengthwise through centers of the hard top shells and the meat. Cut to, but not through, the bottom shells. Using your fingers, spread halves of tails apart slightly.

2 For a charcoal grill, arrange medium-hot coals around a drip pan. Test for medium heat above the pan. Place lobster tails on grill rack over the drip pan. Cover and grill for 25 to 30 minutes or until lobster meat is opaque. (For a gas grill, preheat grill. Reduce heat to medium. Adjust for indirect cooking. Place lobster tails on grill rack over burner that is off. Grill as directed.) Remove lobster. Let cool. Remove meat from tails; discard shells. Cut meat into 1$\frac{1}{2}$-inch pieces.

3 In a small bowl combine the 2 tablespoons oil and the minced garlic. Brush onto cut sides of ciabatta rolls. For a charcoal or gas grill, grill roll halves, cut sides down, on the rack of a covered grill directly over medium heat about 2 minutes or until the bread is crisp and has well-browned grill marks. Transfer to a cutting board. Let cool. Cut into 1-inch cubes.

4 Meanwhile, in a large skillet cook bacon until crisp. Using a slotted spoon, transfer bacon to paper towels. Reserve 1 tablespoon of the bacon drippings. Coarsely chop bacon.

5 For bacon vinaigrette, in a screw-top jar combine the reserved 1 tablespoon bacon drippings, the vinegar, shallot, chives, and 1 tablespoon oil. Cover and shake well to combine.

6 In a large bowl combine spinach, romaine, tomatoes, cucumber, sweet peppers, lobster, and grilled bread cubes. Toss to combine. Transfer to a shallow serving bowl or platter. Drizzle with bacon vinaigrette. Sprinkle with chopped bacon.

QUICK TIP
If you have hearty multgrain or whole grain bread on hand, use it instead of the ciabatta rolls in this panzanella-style salad.

Tuscan Tuna Salad

There is no need to drain the tuna. The oil it is packed in is used as a simple dressing along with lemon peel and juice.

SERVINGS 4 (2 cups each)
CARB. PER SERVING 18 g
START TO FINISH 10 minutes

1 lemon

1 15-ounce can cannellini beans (white kidney beans), rinsed and drained

2 5-ounce cans albacore tuna packed in oil, undrained and broken into chunks

1/2 cup thinly sliced red onion

4 cups arugula or mixed spring greens, lightly packed (5 ounces)

1 cup grape or cherry tomatoes, halved

1/4 teaspoon black pepper

1/8 teaspoon salt

1 | Finely shred 1 teaspoon peel from the lemon. Juice the lemon.

2 | In a large bowl combine cannellini beans, tuna, and onion. Add lemon peel, lemon juice, arugula, and tomatoes; toss to combine. Season with the pepper and salt.

PER SERVING: 204 cal., 4 g total fat (1 g sat. fat), 31 mg chol., 531 mg sodium, 18 g carb. (6 g fiber, 3 g sugars), 21 g pro. Exchanges: 1 vegetable, 1 starch, 2 lean meat.

Greek-Style Orzo and Double-Bean Salad

Take your pick on how to serve this zesty pasta and veggie salad.

SERVINGS 8 (1 cup each)
CARB. PER SERVING 21 g
PREP 20 minutes MARINATE 15 minutes

- ³/₄ cup dried orzo pasta (rosamarina)
- 12 ounces fresh green beans, trimmed and cut into 2-inch pieces
- 1 10-ounce package frozen shelled sweet soybeans (edamame)
- 1 cup grape tomatoes, halved
- ²/₃ cup chopped seedless cucumber
- ¹/₂ cup crumbled feta cheese (2 ounces)
- ¹/₄ cup pitted Kalamata olives, halved
- ¹/₄ cup chopped red onion
- 3 tablespoons red wine vinegar
- 2 tablespoons olive oil
- 2 tablespoons snipped fresh Italian (flat-leaf) parsley
- 2 teaspoons snipped fresh oregano
- 2 teaspoons country Dijon-style mustard
- ¹/₂ teaspoon salt
- ¹/₄ teaspoon black pepper

PER SERVING PLAIN: 187 cal., 8 g total fat (2 g sat. fat), 8 mg chol., 334 mg sodium, 21 g carb. (4 g fiber, 4 g sugars), 8 g pro. Exchanges: 1 vegetable, 1 starch, 1.5 fat.

PER SERVING WITH EGGPLANT: 215 cal., 9 g total fat (2 g sat. fat), 8 mg chol., 481 mg sodium, 26 g carb. (7 g fiber, 7 g sugars), 9 g pro. Exchanges: 2 vegetable, 1 starch, 1.5 fat

PER SERVING WITH PITA CHIPS: 212 cal., 9 g total fat (2 g sat. fat), 8 mg chol., 385 mg sodium, 25 g carb. (4 g fiber, 4 g sugars), 9 g pro. Exchanges: 1 vegetable, 1 starch, 1.5 fat.

TO SERVE SALAD ON GRILLED EGGPLANT: Trim 1 large eggplant and cut crosswise into eight ³/₄-inch slices. Coat both sides with olive oil cooking spray and sprinkle with ¹/₂ teaspoon salt and ¹/₄ teaspoon black pepper. For a charcoal or gas grill, grill eggplant on the rack of a covered grill directly over medium heat for 8 to 10 minutes or until tender, turning once halfway through grilling. Divide grilled eggplant slices among eight dinner plates. Spoon the pasta mixture on top of eggplant.

TO SERVE SALAD WITH PITA CHIPS: Divide the pasta mixture among eight small salad bowls. Divide one 1¹/₂-ounce package unsalted pita chips among the eight servings.

1 | In a large saucepan cook pasta according to package directions, adding green beans and edamame the last 3 minutes of cooking; drain. Rinse with cold water; drain again.

2 | In a large bowl combine pasta mixture, tomatoes, cucumber, cheese, olives, red onion, vinegar, oil, parsley, oregano, mustard, salt, and pepper. Cover and marinate at room temperature for 15 minutes. Chill until ready to serve.

Lentil and Celery Salad with Sautéed Kale and Parmesan Crisps

Kale comes in several varieties; curly kale is the most common found in grocery stores. Any variety works, but expect the flavor to vary.

SERVINGS 6 (^{2}/$_3$ cup salad, ^{2}/$_3$ cup sautéed kale, and, if desired, 1 Parmesan crisp each)
CARB. PER SERVING 28 g
PREP 45 minutes   COOK 25 minutes   BAKE 10 minutes at 350°F

2¼ cups vegetable broth

½ cup water

1 cup French lentils

2 cups sliced celery (4 stalks)

1 cup snipped fresh parsley

3 tablespoons sherry vinegar

2 teaspoons Dijon-style mustard

1 teaspoon packed brown sugar* or agave syrup

2 tablespoons walnut oil or olive oil

3 ounces Parmigiano-Reggiano cheese, finely shredded (optional)

¼ cup chopped onion

2 teaspoons walnut oil or olive oil

8 ounces kale leaves with stems removed (9 to 10 cups loosely packed)

¼ cup dry white wine

¼ teaspoon kosher salt

Pinch black pepper

½ cup chopped walnuts, toasted

1 In a medium saucepan bring broth and the water to boiling. Add lentils; reduce heat. Simmer, covered, for 25 to 30 minutes or until the lentils are tender. Drain off liquid; discard. Stir celery and parsley into cooked lentils. Let stand at room temperature until cool.

2 For dressing, in a small bowl combine sherry vinegar, mustard, and brown sugar. Whisk in the 2 tablespoons oil. For salad, toss together the lentil mixture and dressing. Serve at room temperature or cover and chill up to 24 hours.

3 If making Parmesan crisps, preheat the oven to 350°F. Line a large baking sheet with a silicone baking mat (such as Silpat brand). Spoon shredded cheese onto baking sheet in six mounds, spacing at least 2 inches apart. Using the back of a spoon, pat each mound into a 3-inch circle. Bake for 10 to 13 minutes or until golden. Remove from oven and cool crisps on the baking sheet. Using a metal spatula, carefully remove crisps from baking sheet.

4 Meanwhile, in a very large skillet cook onion in the 2 teaspoons hot oil over medium heat for 3 minutes or until translucent. Add kale, wine, salt, and pepper (skillet will be very full); toss and cook for 2 to 3 minutes or until most of the liquid is absorbed and kale is tender but still vibrant green.

5 Divide salad and kale among six serving plates. Sprinkle with toasted walnuts. If desired, serve with Parmesan crisps.

*SUGAR SUBSTITUTE: Choose Splenda Brown Sugar Blend for Baking. Follow package directions to use product amount equivalent to 1 teaspoon brown sugar.

PER SERVING: 277 cal., 13 g total fat (1 g sat. fat), 0 mg chol., 470 mg sodium, 28 g carb. (12 g fiber, 4 g sugars), 12 g pro. Exchanges: 1 vegetable, 1.5 starch, 0.5 lean meat, 2 fat.

PER SERVING WITH SUBSTITUTE: Same as above, except 276 cal.

Pretzel-Pistachio-Crusted Tofu Salad

Although pistachio nuts offer a unique green color and a distinctive flavor, almonds and pecans are other great nut options.

SERVINGS 4 (1$\frac{1}{2}$ cups salad and 2 tofu slices each)
CARB. PER SERVING 26 g
PREP 20 minutes   COOK 4 minutes

8 ounces extra-firm tofu (fresh bean curd), cut into 8 slices

2 egg whites, lightly beaten

1 ounce unsalted pretzels, crushed ($\frac{1}{4}$ cup)

3 tablespoons finely chopped pistachio nuts

Nonstick cooking spray

5 teaspoons olive oil

2 tablespoons white wine vinegar

2 tablespoons horseradish mustard

1 teaspoon honey

$\frac{1}{4}$ teaspoon salt

6 cups fresh baby spinach

1 medium apple, cored and thinly sliced

$\frac{1}{4}$ cup dried cranberries

1 | Place tofu slices on paper towels; pat dry. Set aside. Place egg whites in a shallow dish. In another shallow dish combine pretzels and nuts. Dip tofu slices in egg whites, turning to coat. Dip tofu slices in pretzel mixture, turning to coat evenly. Coat a very large nonstick skillet with cooking spray. Add 1 teaspoon of the olive oil to the skillet. Heat over medium-high heat. Add tofu slices. Cook for 4 to 6 minutes or until golden and crisp, turning once halfway through cooking time.

2 | For dressing, in a screw-top jar combine the remaining 4 teaspoons oil, the vinegar, mustard, honey, and salt. Cover and shake well.

3 | In a large bowl combine spinach, apple, and cranberries. Divide spinach mixture among four serving plates. Drizzle with dressing. Arrange tofu slices on top. Serve immediately.

12 grams pro.

PER SERVING: 259 cal., 12 g total fat (2 g sat. fat), 0 mg chol., 353 mg sodium, 26 g carb. (5 g fiber, 12 g sugars), 12 g pro. Exchanges: 0.5 vegetable, 1 fruit, 0.5 starch, 1.5 lean meat, 1.5 fat.

QUICK TIP
Horseradish mustard gives the dressing a zesty kick. Use Dijon mustard for a milder version.

comforting
soups and stews

Who can resist a steaming bowl of goodness? Whether it's a

hearty beef stew or a light and simple noodle medley, these

soups fit into a weekday diabetes meal plan. Enjoy them alone

or add a crisp salad to complete the meal.

Beef and Roasted Vegetable Soup

Roasting vegetables before adding them to the soup gives them richer, more concentrated flavors.

SERVINGS 6 (1^1/$_3$ cups each)
CARB. PER SERVING 25 g
PREP 25 minutes   ROAST 45 minutes at 425°F   COOK 25 minutes

1 small butternut squash, cut into ^{3}/$_4$-inch cubes (2^1/$_2$ cups)

8 ounces tiny new potatoes, scrubbed and quartered

2 medium carrots, cut into ^{1}/$_2$-inch pieces

1 large onion, cut into ^{1}/$_2$-inch pieces

1 green sweet pepper, cut into ^{1}/$_2$-inch pieces

3 cloves garlic, minced

2 teaspoons canola oil

1 pound 95% extra-lean ground beef

1 cup no-salt-added diced tomatoes, undrained

8 ounces fresh mushrooms, quartered

32 ounces no-salt-added vegetable stock, such as Kitchen Basics brand

2 sprigs fresh thyme

^{1}/$_2$ teaspoon black pepper

1^1/$_2$ cups shredded kale (2^1/$_2$ ounces)

^{1}/$_4$ cup snipped fresh parsley

1 Preheat oven to 425°F. In a shallow roasting pan arrange squash, potatoes, carrots, onion, sweet pepper, and garlic in a single layer. Drizzle oil over vegetables; toss to coat evenly. Roast for 30 minutes, stirring once.

2 Meanwhile, in a 4-quart Dutch oven cook ground beef over medium heat until meat is browned, using a wooden spoon to break up meat as it cooks; drain off fat. Set meat aside.

3 Add tomatoes and mushrooms to vegetables in roasting pan; roast about 15 minutes more or just until the vegetables are lightly golden.

4 Using a spatula, transfer vegetable mixture to beef in Dutch oven. Return to medium heat; slowly add vegetable stock. Add thyme sprigs and black pepper. Bring to boiling; reduce heat. Simmer, covered, for 20 minutes. Using tongs, remove and discard thyme. Add kale to mixture in Dutch oven. Simmer, covered, for 5 to 10 minutes more or until kale wilts. Stir in parsley. To serve, divide soup among six soup bowls.

25 grams carb.

PER SERVING: 222 cal., 5 g total fat (2 g sat. fat), 46 mg chol., 180 mg sodium, 25 g carb. (5 g fiber, 8 g sugars), 20 g pro. Exchanges: 2 vegetable, 1 starch, 2 lean meat.

Hearty Beef Stew

This satisfying stew combines classic with some healthful changes. Be sure to remove the thyme sprigs and bay leaf before serving.

SERVINGS 6 (1⅓ cups each)
CARB. PER SERVING 16 g
PREP 40 minutes COOK 1 hour 15 minutes

- 2 tablespoons canola oil
- ¼ cup chopped turkey bacon (about 2 slices)
- 1 pound beef stew meat
- ⅛ teaspoon kosher salt or sea salt
- ⅛ teaspoon freshly ground black pepper
- 4 medium carrots, peeled and cut diagonally into 1-inch pieces
- 4 stalks celery, cut diagonally into 1-inch pieces
- 2 large onions, coarsely chopped
- 3 tablespoons tomato paste
- 6 roma tomatoes, coarsely chopped
- 1 cup dry red wine (such as Cabernet Sauvignon) or pomegranate juice
- 2 tablespoons white vinegar
- 2 14.5-ounce cans 50%-less-sodium beef broth
- 3 fresh thyme sprigs
- 1 bay leaf

Fresh thyme sprigs (optional)

1 | In a 4-quart Dutch oven heat oil over medium-high heat. Add bacon; cook about 5 minutes or until browned, stirring occasionally.

2 | Add beef to Dutch oven. Sprinkle with the salt and pepper. Cook about 8 minutes or until browned, stirring occasionally. Remove meat from Dutch oven; set aside.

3 | Add carrots, celery, and onions to Dutch oven. Add tomato paste, stirring to coat vegetables; cook for 2 minutes. Add tomatoes, wine, and vinegar. Bring to boiling, scraping up any browned bits from the bottom of the Dutch oven. Reduce heat. Simmer, uncovered, for 5 minutes. Add broth, the thyme sprigs, the bay leaf, and browned beef mixture. Bring to boiling; reduce heat. Cover and simmer for 45 minutes. Uncover and simmer about 30 minutes more or until thickened and beef and vegetables are tender.

4 | Discard thyme sprigs and bay leaf. To serve, divide stew among six soup bowls. If desired, garnish with additional thyme sprigs.

PER SERVING: 258 cal., 9 g total fat (2 g sat. fat), 38 mg chol., 520 mg sodium, 16 g carb. (4 g fiber, 8 g sugars), 21 g pro. Exchanges: 1.5 vegetable, 0.5 carb., 2.5 lean meat, 1.5 fat.

Easy Chicken Noodle Bowl

If you can't find tiny and tender baby bok choy, go ahead and substitute chopped mature bok choy.

SERVINGS 2 (2 cups each)
CARB. PER SERVING 33 g
START TO FINISH 20 minutes

- 2 ounces rice noodles
- 2 cups unsalted chicken stock
- 4 thin slices peeled fresh ginger
- 1 clove garlic, thinly sliced
- 2 heads baby bok choy (8 ounces)
- 2/3 cup shredded cooked chicken breast
- 1/2 teaspoon fish sauce
- 1/4 cup shredded carrot
- 1/4 cup thinly sliced green onions
- 1 tablespoon snipped fresh basil
- 1 tablespoon snipped fresh mint
- 1 tablespoon snipped fresh cilantro
- 2 lime wedges

Asian chili sauce (Sriracha sauce)

PER SERVING: 242 cal., 2 g total fat (1 g sat. fat), 40 mg chol., 457 mg sodium, 33 g carb. (3 g fiber, 3 g sugars), 22 g pro. Exchanges: 1 vegetable, 1.5 starch, 2 lean meat.

1 Cook rice noodles according to package directions. Drain; rinse with cold water and drain again. Set aside.

2 Meanwhile, in a large saucepan combine chicken stock, ginger, and garlic. Bring to a simmer over medium heat. Cook for 5 minutes. Add bok choy, chicken, and fish sauce. Cook for 2 to 3 minutes or until bok choy is just crisp-tender. Stir in rice noodles, carrot, and green onions. Cook for 1 to 2 minutes more or until noodles are heated through. Remove and discard ginger slices. Stir in basil, mint, and cilantro.

3 To serve, divide noodle mixture between two shallow bowls. Squeeze lime wedges over each serving. Serve with chili sauce to taste.

Wild Rice Chicken Soup

Classic wild rice soup is laden with cream. This version opts for a light broth to bring out the best in flavorful fresh vegetables.

SERVINGS 6 (1 cup each)
CARB. PER SERVING 29 g
PREP 10 minutes COOK 45 minutes

- 2 cups water
- ½ cup uncooked wild rice, rinsed and drained
- ½ cup uncooked long grain brown rice
- 2 14.5-ounce cans reduced-sodium chicken broth
- 4 cloves garlic, minced
- 4 cups chopped tomatoes (8 medium) or two 14.5-ounce cans diced tomatoes, undrained
- 2 cups chopped cooked chicken breast (about 10 ounces)
- 1 cup finely chopped zucchini (1 small)
- ¼ teaspoon freshly ground black pepper
- 1 tablespoon snipped fresh thyme or 1 teaspoon dried thyme, crushed
- 1 tablespoon Madeira wine or dry sherry (optional)

PER SERVING: 218 cal., 3 g total fat (1 g sat. fat), 40 mg chol., 361 mg sodium, 29 g carb. (3 g fiber, 5 g sugars), 21 g pro. Exchanges: 1 vegetable, 1.5 starch, 2 lean meat.

1 In a large saucepan bring the water to boiling. Stir in wild rice and brown rice. Return to boiling; reduce heat. Simmer, covered, 40 to 45 minutes or until rice is tender and most of the liquid is absorbed. Remove from heat.

2 Meanwhile, in a 4-quart Dutch oven combine broth and garlic; bring to boiling. Stir in tomatoes, chicken, zucchini, and pepper. Return to boiling; reduce heat. Simmer, covered, 5 minutes. Stir in cooked rice, thyme, and, if desired, wine; heat through. To serve, divide soup among six soup bowls.

Turkey Avgolemono Soup

Eggs are used to thicken this soup and give it a rich texture. Fresh lemon juice is the key to making it bright and flavorful.

SERVINGS 4 (1½ cups each)
CARB. PER SERVING 15 g
PREP 25 minutes COOK 20 minutes

- ¾ cup chopped red sweet pepper (1 medium)
- 1 medium leek, thinly sliced (white part only) (⅓ cup)
- 1 clove garlic, minced
- 2 teaspoons olive oil
- ½ cup instant brown rice
- 4 cups unsalted chicken stock
- ¼ cup water
- ½ teaspoon salt
- 2 eggs
- 3 tablespoons lemon juice
- 3 cups fresh baby spinach
- 1 cup shredded cooked turkey or chicken breast
- 1 tablespoon snipped fresh dill weed

PER SERVING: 198 cal., 6 g total fat (1 g sat. fat), 121 mg chol., 547 mg sodium, 15 g carb. (2 g fiber, 2 g sugars), 20 g pro. Exchanges: 1 vegetable, 0.5 starch, 2.5 lean meat, 0.5 fat.

1 In a 4-quart Dutch oven cook sweet pepper, leek, and garlic in hot olive oil over medium heat for 3 minutes, stirring occasionally. Add rice; cook and stir for 1 minute. Carefully add chicken stock, water, and salt. Bring to boiling; reduce heat. Simmer, covered, for 10 to 15 minutes or until rice is tender.

2 In a medium bowl whisk together eggs and lemon juice. Gradually stir 1 cup of the hot stock into egg mixture. Stir hot egg mixture into the Dutch oven. Cook and stir for 1 to 2 minutes more or until slightly thickened (do not boil). Stir in spinach, turkey, and dill. Heat through. To serve, divide soup among four soup bowls.

Peanut and Shrimp Soup

A variety of spices and flavorings blend harmoniously to give rich flavor to a surprisingly simple squash soup.

SERVINGS 8 (1 cup soup, $^1/_4$ cup carrots, and 2 or 3 shrimp each)
CARB. PER SERVING 24 g
PREP 55 minutes ROAST 35 minutes at 450°F COOK 30 minutes

1 pound fresh or frozen large shrimp

1 2$^1/_4$- to 2$^1/_2$-pound butternut squash,* halved and seeded

2 teaspoons ground cumin

$^3/_4$ teaspoon kosher salt

$^1/_2$ teaspoon black pepper

$^1/_2$ teaspoon ground coriander

$^1/_4$ teaspoon ground cinnamon

$^1/_4$ teaspoon ground turmeric

2 teaspoons toasted sesame oil

1 cup chopped onion (1 large)

$^1/_2$ of a large red sweet pepper, coarsely chopped

2 teaspoons finely chopped fresh jalapeño chile pepper**

3 cloves garlic, minced

1 tablespoon grated fresh ginger

2 tablespoons mlld green curry paste

1 teaspoon reduced-sodium soy sauce

2 14.5-ounce cans no-salt-added petite diced tomatoes, undrained

$^3/_4$ cup creamy peanut butter

3 cups low-sodium vegetable broth, such as Pacific brand

Nonstick cooking spray

2 cups packaged fresh julienned carrots***

PER SERVING: 276 cal., 14 g total fat (3 g sat. fat), 79 mg chol., 584 mg sodium, 24 g carb. (7 g fiber, 11 g sugars), 18 g pro. Exchanges: 1.5 starch, 2 lean meat, 1 fat.

1 | Thaw shrimp, if frozen. Peel and devein shrimp. Rinse shrimp; pat dry with paper towels. Preheat oven to 450°F. Grease a 15×10×1-inch baking pan; place squash, cut sides down, in pan. Roast for 35 to 45 minutes or until tender when pierced with a fork. Cool slightly. Scoop pulp from shells; mash (you should have about 2 cups mashed squash).

2 | In a small bowl combine cumin, salt, black pepper, coriander, cinnamon, and turmeric. Place shrimp in a medium bowl. Sprinkle 2 teaspoons of the spice mixture over shrimp; stir. Cover and refrigerate while you prepare the soup.

3 | For soup, in a 4- to 5-quart Dutch oven heat sesame oil over medium heat. Add onion, sweet pepper, chile pepper, garlic, and ginger; cook about 5 minutes or until tender. Add curry paste, soy sauce, and the remaining spice mixture. Stir in mashed squash, tomatoes, and peanut butter. Stir in vegetable broth. Bring to boiling; reduce heat. Simmer, covered, 30 minutes.

4 | Meanwhile, lightly coat a very large nonstick or heavy cast-iron skillet or grill pan with cooking spray. Heat over medium-high heat. Add shrimp in a single layer. Cook for 5 minutes or until shrimp are opaque, turning once. In a saucepan cook carrots in a small amount of boiling water for 4 to 5 minutes or just until tender; drain.

5 | To serve, divide soup among eight soup bowls. Top with carrots and shrimp.

*TEST KITCHEN TIP: If you prefer, substitute 2 cups thawed frozen cooked winter squash for the butternut squash; omit roasting the squash in Step 1.

**TEST KITCHEN TIP: Because chile peppers contain volatile oils that can burn your skin and eyes, avoid direct contact with them as much as possible. When working with chile peppers, wear plastic or rubber gloves. If your bare hands do touch the peppers, wash your hands and nails well with soap and warm water.

***TEST KITCHEN TIP: If you prefer, prepare your own julienne carrots by peeling about 4 medium carrots and cutting them into matchstick-size pieces.

Tomato and Bean Soup

Baked corn tortilla strips add a crunchy topping that is a more healthful option to crushed corn chips.

>> SERVINGS 2 (1¼ cups soup and ½ tortilla each)
CARB. PER SERVING 31 g
START TO FINISH 45 minutes

1 teaspoon olive oil

½ small sweet potato, peeled and finely chopped (½ cup)

2 tablespoons chopped shallot

½ fresh jalapeño chile pepper, seeded and sliced,* or 1 canned chipotle chile, finely chopped

¼ teaspoon chili powder

1 cup reduced-sodium chicken broth or vegetable broth

1 5.5-ounce can hot-style tomato juice

½ cup no-salt-added canned black beans, rinsed and drained

½ cup quartered grape or cherry tomatoes

1 5-inch corn tortilla

Nonstick cooking spray

2 teaspoons snipped fresh chives

2 lemon wedges

PER SERVING: 173 cal., 3 g total fat (0 g sat. fat), 0 mg chol., 472 mg sodium, 31 g carb. (8 g fiber, 7 g sugars), 8 g pro. Exchanges: 1.5 vegetable, 1.5 starch, 0.5 fat.

1 Preheat oven to 375°F. In a medium nonstick saucepan heat oil over medium-high heat. Add sweet potato, shallot, jalapeño pepper, and chili powder. Cook and stir about 4 minutes or until shallot is tender. Add broth, tomato juice, and beans. Bring to boiling; reduce heat. Simmer, covered, about 8 minutes or until sweet potato is tender, stirring occasionally. Stir in tomatoes; cook for 2 minutes.

2 Meanwhile, lightly coat tortilla with cooking spray. Cut into thin strips. Spread strips on a small baking sheet. Bake for 6 to 8 minutes or until crisp and light brown on the edges.

3 To serve, divide soup between two soup bowls. Top with tortilla strips and chives. Serve with lemon wedges.

*TEST KITCHEN TIP: Because chile peppers contain volatile oils that can burn your skin and eyes, avoid direct contact with them as much as possible. When working with chile peppers, wear plastic or rubber gloves. If your bare hands do touch the peppers, wash your hands and nails well with soap and warm water.

Italian-Style Lentil Soup

Adding the tomatoes to this soup at the end allows the lentils to cook completely.

SERVINGS 6 (1 1/3 cups each)
CARB. PER SERVING 42 g
PREP 25 minutes COOK 40 minutes

- 1 tablespoon olive oil or canola oil
- 1/2 cup chopped onion (1 medium)
- 6 cloves garlic, minced, or 1 tablespoon bottled minced garlic
- 1 32-ounce box reduced-sodium chicken broth (4 cups)
- 2 cups water
- 1 cup dry brown lentils
- 1 1/2 teaspoons dried Italian seasoning, crushed
- 1/2 teaspoon black pepper
- 1 14.5-ounce can no-salt-added diced tomatoes, undrained
- 1 6-ounce can no-salt-added tomato paste
- 2 cups frozen peas and carrots
- 2 ounces dried multigrain penne pasta or multigrain elbow macaroni
- 1/4 cup finely shredded Parmesan cheese (optional)

1 In a large saucepan or 4-quart Dutch oven heat oil over medium heat. Add onion and garlic; cook about 5 minutes or until onion is tender, stirring occasionally.

2 Add broth, the water, lentils, Italian seasoning, and pepper to onion mixture. Bring to boiling; reduce heat. Cover and simmer for 30 minutes.

3 Stir in tomatoes and tomato paste. Stir in peas and carrots and uncooked pasta. Return to boiling; reduce heat. Simmer, uncovered, about 10 minutes or until pasta is tender.

4 To serve, divide soup among six soup bowls. If desired, sprinkle with Parmesan cheese.

PER SERVING: 251 cal., 3 g total fat (0 g sat. fat), 0 mg chol., 467 mg sodium, 42 g carb. (15 g fiber, 8 g sugars), 15 g pro. Exchanges: 1 vegetable, 2.5 starch, 1 lean meat.

Farro-Vegetable Soup

Use reduced-sodium or no-salt-added products in soup to give yourself the greatest control over the saltiness.

SERVINGS 6 (1³/₄ cups each)
CARB. PER SERVING 34 g
PREP 30 minutes COOK 25 minutes

½ cup pearled farro, rinsed

1 medium bulb fennel, trimmed and sliced (2 cups)

2 cups sliced fresh cremini or button mushrooms

1 cup chopped carrots (2 medium)

½ cup chopped onion (1 medium)

2 cloves garlic, thinly sliced

1 tablespoon olive oil

6 cups low-sodium vegetable broth or 50%-less-sodium beef broth

1 15-ounce can cannellini beans (white kidney beans), rinsed and drained

1 14.5-ounce can no-salt-added diced tomatoes, undrained

1 small zucchini, halved lengthwise and sliced (1 cup)

1½ teaspoons dried Italian seasoning, crushed

¾ teaspoon salt

¼ teaspoon black pepper

Shaved Parmesan cheese (optional)

Fennel fronds (optional)

1 Cook farro according to package directions. Drain; set aside.

2 Meanwhile, in a large Dutch oven cook fennel, mushrooms, carrots, onion, and garlic in hot olive oil over medium heat for 10 minutes, stirring occasionally. Stir in broth, cannellini beans, tomatoes, and zucchini. Bring to boiling; reduce heat. Simmer, covered, for 10 to 15 minutes or until vegetables are tender. Stir in cooked farro, Italian seasoning, salt, and pepper.

3 To serve, divide soup among six soup bowls. If desired, top with Parmesan cheese and fennel fronds.

3 grams fat

PER SERVING: 193 cal., 3 g total fat (0 g sat. fat), 0 mg chol., 511 mg sodium, 34 g carb. (9 g fiber, 7 g sugars), 8 g pro. Exchanges: 2 vegetable, 1.5 starch, 0.5 fat.

QUICK TIP
Farro is the Italian name for emmer,
an ancient strain of wheat. It is used in
soups the same ways as barley.

4

sensational
sandwiches

Sandwiches are the go-to when you want a satisfying lunch

for yourself or need to make a quick dinner for the family.

Enjoy some new takes on old favorites that are built with great

ingredients and good health in mind.

Open-Face Philly-Style Chicken Sandwiches

An easy way to cut the carbs is to enjoy hot sandwiches open-face. Dig in with a knife and fork.

SERVINGS 6 (1 sandwich each)
CARB. PER SERVING 26 g
START TO FINISH 30 minutes

- 1 tablespoon olive oil
- 1¼ pounds skinless, boneless chicken breast halves, cut into thin strips
- 2 cups thinly sliced onions
- 1 cup green, red, and/or yellow sweet pepper strips
- 1 to 2 cloves garlic, minced
- 1 teaspoon dried Italian seasoning, crushed
- ½ teaspoon black pepper
- 6 slices reduced-fat provolone cheese (4 ounces)
- 6 ½-inch-thick slices whole grain bread (9 ounces)

1 Preheat broiler. In a large skillet heat oil over medium-high heat. Add the chicken; cook and stir about 5 minutes or until no longer pink. Reduce heat to medium. Add the onion slices, pepper strips, garlic, Italian seasoning, and black pepper. Cook and stir for 5 to 8 minutes or until vegetables are tender. Reduce heat to low. Place the cheese slices in a single layer over the chicken mixture. Cover and cook about 1 minute more or until the cheese is melted.

2 Meanwhile, arrange bread on a baking sheet. Broil bread 4 to 5 inches from the heat for 1 to 2 minutes per side or until toasted. Using a spatula, transfer portions of cheese-topped chicken mixture onto toasted bread slices.

PER SERVING: 321 cal., 10 g total fat (3 g sat. fat), 71 mg chol., 435 mg sodium, 26 g carb. (5 g fiber, 6 g sugars), 31 g pro. Exchanges: 1 vegetable, 1.5 starch, 3.5 lean meat, 0.5 fat.

QUICK TIP
Philly sandwiches typically use only green sweet peppers. Because these are open-face sandwiches, make them pretty with three different colors.

Southwestern Cherry-Oat Chicken Sandwiches

Using rolled oats and dried cherries to coat chicken breasts gives them a delightful crunchy-chewy texture.

SERVINGS 4 (1 sandwich each)
CARB. PER SERVING 36 g or 35 g
PREP 30 minutes
BAKE 15 minutes at 425°F

- 2 tablespoons light mayonnaise
- ½ teaspoon finely chopped canned chipotle chile peppers in adobo sauce (see tip, *page 80*)
- ½ teaspoon sugar*
- ½ teaspoon lime juice
- Nonstick cooking spray
- 2 skinless, boneless chicken breast halves (about 1 pound total)
- ¼ cup plain fat-free Greek yogurt
- 1 tablespoon water
- ½ cup soft whole wheat bread crumbs
- ¼ cup regular rolled oats
- 3 tablespoons finely chopped dried cherries
- 4 whole wheat sandwich thins, such as Oroweat brand, toasted
- 4 to 8 lettuce leaves
- 4 slices tomato
- 8 slices lower-sodium and less-fat bacon, cooked
- 4 thin red onion slices (optional)

PER SERVING: 361 cal., 9 g total fat (2 g sat. fat), 80 mg chol., 567 mg sodium, 36 g carb. (7 g fiber, 9 g sugars), 36 g pro. Exchanges: 0.5 fruit, 1.5 starch, 4.5 lean meat, 1 fat.

PER SERVING WITH SUBSTITUTE: Same as above, except 359 cal., 35 g carb. (8 g sugars).

1 | In a small bowl combine mayonnaise, chile peppers, sugar, and lime juice; set aside.

2 | Preheat oven to 425°F. Line a baking sheet with foil; coat foil with cooking spray and set aside. Cut chicken breasts in half lengthwise. In a shallow dish combine yogurt and the water. In another shallow dish combine bread crumbs, oats, and dried cherries. Dip chicken pieces in yogurt mixture, turning to coat. Dip in bread crumb mixture, turning to coat evenly.

3 | Place chicken on prepared baking sheet. Bake for 15 to 18 minutes or until chicken is no longer pink (165°F) and outside is golden brown.

4 | To serve, spread mayonnaise mixture on cut sides of sandwich thin tops. Place lettuce on cut sides of sandwich thin bottoms; top with chicken, tomato, bacon, and, if desired, onion slices. Add tops of sandwich thins, mayonnaise sides down.

*SUGAR SUBSTITUTES: Choose from Splenda Granular, Truvia Spoonable or packets, or Sweet'N Low bulk or packets. Follow package directions to use product amount equivalent to ½ teaspoon sugar.

QUICK TIP

Save time when preparing these wraps by purchasing packaged shredded broccoli or broccoli slaw mix.

Turkey Lettuce Wraps with Peanut Sauce

Ditch the bread and wrap your sandwich in a lettuce leaf. Boston and Bibb varieties work best to cradle the sandwich filling.

SERVINGS 8 (1 wrap each)
CARB. PER SERVING 12 g or 9 g
PREP 15 minutes COOK 20 minutes

- 1 pound uncooked ground turkey
- 1 tablespoon grated fresh ginger
- 3 cloves garlic, minced
- 1 teaspoon five-spice powder or curry powder
- 2 cups small broccoli florets or coarsely shredded broccoli (1 small bunch)*
- 1 small red onion, thinly sliced
- $3/4$ teaspoon salt
- $1/2$ teaspoon black pepper
- 8 large Boston or Bibb lettuce leaves (about 2 heads)
- 1 recipe Peanut Sauce or $1/2$ cup hoisin sauce
- 8 lime wedges
- Snipped fresh cilantro (optional)

PER SERVING: 198 cal., 12 g total fat (3 g sat. fat), 44 mg chol., 290 mg sodium, 12 g carb. (2 g fiber, 8 g sugars), 12 g pro. Exchanges: 1 vegetable, 0.5 carb., 1.5 lean meat, 2 fat.

PER SERVING WITH SUBSTITUTE: Same as above, except 189 cal., 9 g carb. (5 g sugars).

1 | In a large nonstick skillet cook turkey over medium-high heat for 5 minutes, breaking up turkey with a wooden spoon as it cooks. Stir in ginger, garlic, and $1/2$ teaspoon of the five-spice powder; cook about 5 minutes more or until turkey is no longer pink. Using a slotted spoon, transfer turkey mixture to a bowl; set aside.

2 | In the same skillet cook broccoli, onion, and the remaining $1/2$ teaspoon five-spice powder about 4 minutes or just until broccoli and onion are tender. Stir in the turkey mixture; heat through. Season with the salt and pepper.

3 | To serve, divide turkey-broccoli mixture among lettuce leaves. Spoon about 1 tablespoon Peanut Sauce on top of the filling in each wrap. Squeeze a lime wedge over the sauce on each wrap. If desired, top with cilantro. Fold in the two opposite sides of the lettuce leaf. Serve immediately.

PEANUT SAUCE: In a small saucepan combine $1/4$ cup sugar,** 3 tablespoons crunchy peanut butter, 2 tablespoons water, and 1 tablespoon vegetable oil. Heat over medium-low heat just until bubbly and mixture looks smooth (it may look curdled before this stage), stirring frequently. Season to taste with $1/4$ to $1/2$ teaspoon Asian chili sauce.

*TEST KITCHEN TIP: If using shredded broccoli, you can peel the stalks, especially if they seem tough. Shred broccoli in a food processor fitted with a coarse shredding blade or use a manual shredder.

**SUGAR SUBSTITUTE: Choose Splenda Sugar Blend for Baking. Follow package directions to use product amount equivalent to $1/4$ cup sugar.

Ham and Grape Grilled Cheese

A burst of sweet, juicy grapes gives an unexpected twist to a classic sandwich.

>> SERVINGS 4 (1 sandwich each)
CARB. PER SERVING 31 g
START TO FINISH 20 minutes

1½ cups seedless red grapes, coarsely chopped

8 slices thin slices marble rye bread (6 ounces total)

2 ounces low-fat, reduced-sodium, thinly sliced cooked ham

Nonstick cooking spray

4 ultrathin slices Swiss cheese

1 | In a large nonstick skillet cook grapes over medium heat 2 to 4 minutes or just until grapes are softened. Drain off any liquid.

2 | Layer four of the bread slices with ham, grapes, and cheese. Top with the remaining four bread slices. Lightly coat outsides of sandwiches with cooking spray.

3 | Rinse and dry the skillet. Preheat skillet over medium heat. Place sandwiches, half at a time if necessary, in skillet. Cook for 2 to 3 minutes or until bread is toasted. Turn sandwiches and cook for 1 to 2 minutes more or until bread is toasted and filling is heated through. Serve immediately.

QUICK TIP
Start grilling sandwiches cheese sides down. The cheese will melt and hold the grapes in place, making it easier to turn the sandwiches without any grapes falling out.

PER SERVING: 213 cal., 6 g total fat (2 g sat. fat), 18 mg chol., 417 mg sodium, 31 g carb. (3 g fiber, 10 g sugars), 10 g pro. Exchanges: 0.5 fruit, 1.5 starch, 1 lean meat, 0.5 fat.

Shrimp and Pineapple Lettuce Cups

Turn a salad into a sandwich. Instead of spooning the shrimp mixture over shredded lettuce, spoon it into cupped lettuce leaves.

SERVINGS 4 (1¹/₄ cups each)
CARB. PER SERVING 11 g
START TO FINISH 20 minutes

1 pound fresh peeled, deveined cooked shrimp

1¹/₂ cups chopped fresh pineapple

1 cup chopped red sweet pepper

¹/₂ cup snipped fresh cilantro

2 teaspoons toasted sesame oil

¹/₄ teaspoon salt

¹/₄ teaspoon black pepper

1 head Boston or Bibb lettuce, leaves separated

1 Coarsely chop shrimp if desired. In a medium bowl stir together shrimp, pineapple, sweet pepper, cilantro, and sesame oil. Season with the salt and black pepper. To serve, spoon shrimp mixture into lettuce leaves.

PER SERVING: 179 cal., 3 g total fat (0 g sat. fat), 214 mg chol., 276 mg sodium, 11 g carb. (2 g fiber, 8 g sugars), 28 g pro. Exchanges: 0.5 vegetable, 0.5 starch, 4 lean meat.

Black Bean-Queso Wraps

Grilled wraps? You bet! Just make sure to fold the sides of the tortillas in when making the sandwiches to hold everything in place.

>> SERVINGS 4 (1 wrap each)
CARB. PER SERVING 28 g
START TO FINISH 20 minutes

½ cup chopped red sweet pepper (1 small)

¼ cup chopped poblano chile pepper*

2 teaspoons canola oil

⅓ cup thinly sliced green onions

⅓ cup canned reduced-sodium black beans, rinsed and drained

⅓ cup frozen whole kernel corn, thawed

2 tablespoons snipped fresh cilantro

2 tablespoons salsa verde

4 8-inch whole wheat low-carb flour tortillas

1 cup shredded queso Oaxaca or Monterey Jack cheese (4 ounces)

Nonstick cooking spray

1 | In a medium skillet cook sweet pepper and poblano pepper in hot oil over medium heat for 3 to 5 minutes or until crisp-tender, stirring occasionally. Stir in green onions. Remove from heat. Stir in beans, corn, cilantro, and salsa verde.

2 | Place tortillas between paper towels. Microwave on 100 percent power (high) for 20 to 40 seconds or until warm. Spoon bean mixture onto tortillas just below centers. Top with cheese. Fold bottom edge of each tortilla up and over filling. Fold in opposite sides; roll up from the bottom. Lightly coat outsides of wraps with cooking spray.

3 | Preheat a panini grill according to the manufacturer's directions. Place wraps, half at a time if necessary, in grill. Close lid and grill for 2 to 3 minutes or until tortillas are toasted and filling is heated through. (Or use a skillet to heat the wraps. Place wraps in a preheated skillet; place a large skillet on top of wraps. You may need to add a few unopened cans of food to the top skillet for extra weight. Cook for 2 to 3 minutes or until golden brown on bottoms. Carefully remove top skillet [it may be hot]. Turn wraps. Replace skillet and weights; cook for 2 to 3 minutes more or until wraps are golden and heated through.)

*TEST KITCHEN TIP: Because chile peppers contain volatile oils that can burn your skin and eyes, avoid direct contact with them as much as possible. When working with chile peppers, wear plastic or rubber gloves. If your bare hands do touch the peppers, wash your hands and nails well with soap and warm water.

17 grams pro.

PER SERVING: 233 cal., 12 g total fat (0 g sat. fat), 24 mg chol., 388 mg sodium, 28 g carb. (14 g fiber, 3 g sugars), 17 g pro. Exchanges: 0.5 vegetable, 1.5 starch, 1.5 lean meat, 1.5 fat.

Hummus and Avocado Salad Sandwiches

Perfectly ripe avocado joins rich-flavored hummus in these creamy-meets-creamy sandwiches. Arugula adds a peppery bite.

SERVINGS 4 (1 sandwich each)
CARB. PER SERVING 26 g
START TO FINISH 25 minutes

Nonstick cooking spray

⅓ cup Mediterranean-flavor hummus, such as Sabra Tuscan Herb brand*

4 whole wheat sandwich thins or bagel bread squares, split

¼ teaspoon black pepper

½ of an avocado, peeled and sliced

1 cup arugula leaves

2 ounces Gruyère cheese, shredded (½ cup)

PER SERVING: 235 cal., 12 g total fat (3 g sat. fat), 16 mg chol., 354 mg sodium, 26 g carb. (8 g fiber, 3 g sugars), 11 g pro. Exchanges: 1.5 starch, 1 lean meat, 2 fat.

1 | Lightly coat an unheated panini grill, covered indoor electric grill, or large nonstick skillet with cooking spray. Heat grill according to manufacturer's directions or heat skillet over medium heat.

2 | Spread the hummus on cut sides of sandwich thins. Sprinkle with pepper. Divide avocado slices among sandwich thin bottoms. For each sandwich, top avocado slices with ¼ cup of the arugula leaves and 2 tablespoons of the shredded cheese. Place sandwich thin tops on the cheese, spread sides down. Press down lightly.

3 | Place sandwiches on grill or skillet, adding in batches if necessary. If using grill, close lid and grill for 2 to 3 minutes or until bread is toasted. (If using skillet, place a heavy saucepan or skillet on top of sandwiches. Cook about 2 minutes or until bottoms are toasted. Carefully remove saucepan or top skillet [it may be hot]. Turn sandwiches; top again with the saucepan or skillet. Cook about 2 minutes more or until bread is toasted.)

*TEST KITCHEN TIP: To keep sodium in check, read nutrition labels and choose a hummus that has no more than 120 mg sodium per serving.

Grilled Pear-Cheddar Pocket

This quick grilled pocket sandwich makes a perfect light but satisfying lunch

SERVINGS 1 (1 pocket sandwich)
CARB. PER SERVING 29 g
START TO FINISH 15 minutes

2 teaspoons Dijon-style mustard

1/2 of a whole grain pocket thin flatbread, such as Brownberry brand

2 slices ultrathin sharp or mild cheddar cheese, such as Sargento brand

1/4 cup arugula

1/3 of a medium red pear, cored and cut into 1/4-inch-thick slices

QUICK TIP
Munch on the leftover pear for this sandwich while you tend to the grilling.

PER SERVING: 223 cal., 9 g total fat (4 g sat. fat), 20 mg chol., 552 mg sodium, 29 g carb. (7 g fiber, 8 g sugars), 11 g pro. Exchanges: 0.5 vegetable, 0.5 fruit, 1 starch, 1 medium-fat meat, 1 fat.

1 Preheat a small covered indoor electric grill or nonstick skillet. Spread mustard over the interior surfaces of the pocket thin flatbread half. Arrange the cheese slices in the pocket, folding to fit. Add arugula and pear slices.

2 Place the flatbread half on the preheated grill and close lid. Grill about 1 1/2 minutes or until lightly toasted. (If using a skillet, place filled pocket in the preheated skillet and cook for 2 to 4 minutes or until lightly toasted, turning pocket once.)

Caprese Panini

It's a classic sandwich and salad pairing all in one. Make this when garden-fresh tomatoes are at their best.

SERVINGS 4 (1 sandwich each)
CARB. PER SERVING 23 g
START TO FINISH 25 minutes

8 slices whole wheat bread

Nonstick olive oil cooking spray

2 medium tomatoes, thinly sliced

4 ounces fresh mozzarella cheese, cut into 4 slices

½ cup fresh basil leaves

Balsamic vinegar (optional)

1 | Coat one side of each bread slice with cooking spray. Place bread slices, coated sides down, on a work surface. Arrange tomatoes, mozzarella cheese, and basil on four of the bread slices. Top with the remaining four bread slices, coated sides up; press together gently.

2 | Heat a covered indoor electric grill, panini grill, grill pan, or large skillet. Place sandwiches, half at a time if necessary, in grill or panini grill. Close lid and grill for 3 to 4 minutes or until bread is toasted and cheese is melted. (If using a grill pan or skillet, place a heavy saucepan or skillet on top of sandwiches. Cook for 2 to 3 minutes or until bread is toasted. Carefully remove saucepan or top skillet [it may be hot]. Turn sandwiches; top again with the saucepan or skillet. Cook about 2 minutes more or until bread is toasted and cheese is melted.) Serve immediately. If desired, serve with balsamic vinegar for dipping.

7 grams fat

PER SERVING: 208 cal., 7 g total fat (3 g sat. fat), 20 mg chol., 288 mg sodium, 23 g carb. (4 g fiber, 4 g sugars), 12 g pro. Exchanges: 1.5 starch, 1 medium-fat meat.

simple
sides and salads

Need something to make a simple main dish like grilled meat

or poultry a great meal? Give your everyday menus a lift with

these fresh and flavorful meal accompaniments. Each is loaded

with nutrition goodness and is perfect for rounding out your

meal plans.

Raspberry Corn Salad

Use a spatula to gently fold the salad mixture so the raspberries and avocado pieces keep their shape.

SERVINGS 6 (³/₄ cup each)
CARB. PER SERVING 15 g
START TO FINISH 25 minutes

- 3 tablespoons lime juice
- 1 tablespoon olive oil
- ½ teaspoon salt
- ⅛ teaspoon black pepper
- 3 ears corn or 2½ cups frozen whole kernel corn, thawed
- 4 medium radishes, trimmed and very thinly sliced, or 1 medium fresh poblano chile pepper, seeded and cut into thin bite-size strips*
- ¼ cup thinly sliced green onions (2)
- ¼ cup snipped fresh cilantro
- 1½ cups fresh raspberries
- 1 medium avocado, halved, seeded, peeled, and coarsely chopped

1 In a medium bowl whisk together lime juice, oil, salt, and black pepper. If using ears of corn, cut kernels from cobs. Add corn, radishes or chile pepper, green onions, and cilantro to lime mixture. Toss until well coated. Add raspberries and avocado just before serving; fold gently to combine. Serve immediately.

***TEST KITCHEN TIP:** Because chile peppers contain volatile oils that can burn your skin and eyes, avoid direct contact with them as much as possible. When working with chile peppers, wear plastic or rubber gloves. If your bare hands do touch the peppers, wash your hands and nails well with soap and warm water.

PER SERVING: 116 cal., 7 g total fat (1 g sat. fat), 0 mg chol., 205 mg sodium, 15 g carb. (5 g fiber, 5 g sugars), 2 g pro. Exchanges: 1 starch, 1 fat.

Fresh Corn Cakes with Cilantro Cream

Pop the first batch of cooked corn cakes into a 300°F oven to keep them warm while cooking the next batch..

SERVINGS 6 (2 corn cakes and 2$\frac{1}{2}$ tablespoons cilantro cream each)
CARB. PER SERVING 27 g
START TO FINISH 35 minutes

- $\frac{1}{2}$ cup whole wheat panko bread crumbs
- $\frac{1}{2}$ cup cornmeal
- $\frac{1}{4}$ teaspoon salt
- $\frac{1}{4}$ cup fat-free milk
- 2 eggs, lightly beaten
- 2 egg whites, lightly beaten
- 2 cups fresh corn kernels (4 ears)
- $\frac{1}{2}$ cup finely shredded carrot (1 medium)
- $\frac{1}{2}$ cup finely chopped green sweet pepper (1 small)
- Nonstick cooking spray
- 2 teaspoons olive oil
- 1 recipe Cilantro Cream

1 In a large bowl stir together panko, cornmeal, and salt. Whisk in milk, eggs, and egg whites until combined. Stir in corn, carrot, and sweet pepper.

2 Coat a very large nonstick skillet with cooking spray; brush with 1 teaspoon of the oil. Heat over medium-high heat. Using a $\frac{1}{4}$-cup measure, add six portions of the corn mixture to the hot skillet, spacing evenly. Cook about 6 minutes or until golden brown, turning once. Transfer cooked corn cakes to a warm serving plate. Repeat with the remaining 1 teaspoon oil and the remaining corn mixture. Serve with Cilantro Cream.

CILANTRO CREAM: In a small bowl whisk together $\frac{3}{4}$ cup finely snipped fresh cilantro, 2 tablespoons thinly sliced green onion (1), 4 teaspoons lime juice, and 2 teaspoons fat-free milk. Whisk in one 6-ounce carton plain low-fat Greek yogurt.

PER SERVING: 187 cal., 5 g total fat (1 g sat. fat), 64 mg chol., 178 mg sodium, 27 g carb. (3 g fiber, 6 g sugars), 10 g pro.
Exchanges: 1 vegetable, 1.5 starch, 1 lean meat.

QUICK TIP
Cook these crispy cakes in two batches so you don't crowd the skillet. Carefully turn the cakes when the first side is golden.

QUICK TIP
For a mild version of this fresh and tasty potato salad, substitute chopped green sweet pepper for the jalapeño pepper.

New Potato Salad with Cucumber and Jalapeño

If you have dried dill weed in the cupboard, use 1 teaspoon of it in place of the fresh.

SERVINGS 8 (³⁄₄ cup each)
CARB. PER SERVING 17 g
PREP 30 minutes **COOK** 12 minutes **CHILL** 2 hours

1½ pounds red or multicolor tiny new potatoes
1 6-ounce carton plain low-fat Greek yogurt
2 tablespoons white balsamic vinegar
1 tablespoon yellow mustard
1 tablespoon honey
1 tablespoon snipped fresh dill weed
¼ teaspoon salt
⅛ teaspoon black pepper
2 cups chopped, seeded cucumber
¾ cup chopped red onion
¼ cup chopped or sliced fresh jalapeño chile pepper*
2 hard-cooked eggs, chopped
Fresh dill (optional)

1 Halve any large potatoes. In a covered large saucepan cook potatoes in enough boiling water to cover for 12 to 15 minutes or just until tender. Drain well. Cool completely. Cut potatoes into halves or quarters.

2 In a large bowl combine yogurt, vinegar, mustard, honey, the snipped dill, the salt, and black pepper. Stir in cucumber, red onion, and jalapeño pepper. Add the cooked potatoes and eggs; gently toss to coat. Cover and chill for at least 2 hours or up to 4 hours. Toss before serving. If desired, garnish with additional dill.

*TEST KITCHEN TIP: Because chile peppers contain volatile oils that can burn your skin and eyes, avoid direct contact with them as much as possible. When working with chile peppers, wear plastic or rubber gloves. If your bare hands do touch the peppers, wash your hands and nails well with soap and warm water.

PER SERVING: 107 cal., 2 g total fat (1 g sat. fat), 48 mg chol., 129 mg sodium, 17 g carb. (2 g fiber, 7 g sugars), 5 g pro. Exchanges: 1 starch, 0.5 fat.

2 grams fat

Tomato and Kale Pesto Pasta

Is your grape tomato plant bursting with the small nuggets of sweetness?
If so, substitute halved grape tomatoes in place of chopped tomatoes.

SERVINGS 8 (³/4 cup each)
CARB. PER SERVING 21 g
START TO FINISH 25 minutes

2 cups fresh baby kale (2 ounces)

½ cup fresh basil leaves

⅓ cup canned reduced-sodium garbanzo beans (chickpeas)

1½ ounces Parmesan cheese, finely shredded

2 tablespoons lemon juice

2 tablespoons olive oil

3 cloves garlic, quartered

¼ teaspoon salt

¼ teaspoon black pepper

6 ounces whole grain penne pasta

3 cups chopped, seeded tomatoes (6 medium)

Shaved Parmesan cheese (optional)

1 For pesto, in a food processor combine kale, basil, garbanzo beans, shredded Parmesan cheese, lemon juice, oil, garlic, salt, and pepper. Cover and pulse with three or four on/off turns until starting to mix; process until finely chopped, scraping down sides as necessary.

2 Meanwhile, cook pasta according to package directions. Drain well. Stir pesto into hot pasta. Fold tomatoes into pasta mixture. If desired, garnish with shaved Parmesan cheese. Serve warm or at room temperature.

PER SERVING: 154 cal., 6 g total fat (1 g sat. fat), 4 mg chol., 177 mg sodium, 21 g carb. (4 g fiber, 3 g sugars), 6 g pro. Exchanges: 1 vegetable, 1 starch, 1 fat.

Fresh Bean Salad

A quick plunge in cold water helps stop the cooking of the beans and preserves the vivid green color.

>> SERVINGS 8 (³/₄ cup each)
CARB. PER SERVING 13 g
PREP 30 minutes CHILL 2 hours

- 1 pound fresh green beans and/or wax beans
- 2 tablespoons water
- 1¹/₃ cups chopped red sweet pepper (1 large)
- 1 10-ounce package frozen shelled sweet soybeans (edamame), cooked according to package directions and cooled
- ¹/₂ cup sliced green onions (4)
- 1 large clove garlic, minced
- 2 tablespoons canola oil
- 2 tablespoons honey
- 2 tablespoons lime juice
- ¹/₂ teaspoon chili powder
- ¹/₈ teaspoon salt
- 1 to 2 dashes bottled hot pepper sauce

PER SERVING: 111 cal., 5 g total fat (0 g sat. fat), 0 mg chol., 46 mg sodium, 13 g carb. (4 g fiber, 8 g sugars), 5 g pro. Exchanges: 1 vegetable, 0.5 starch, 1 fat.

1 | Snap each bean into two or three pieces. In a microwave-safe dish combine beans and the water; cover. Microwave on 100 percent power (high) for 6 to 7 minutes or just until beans are crisp-tender and bright green, stirring once. Drain. Rinse well with cold water; drain well.

2 | In a large bowl toss green beans with sweet pepper, edamame, and green onions.

3 | For dressing, in a screw-top jar combine garlic, oil, honey, lime juice, chili powder, salt, and hot pepper sauce. Cover and shake well. Pour dressing over vegetables; toss to combine. Chill for at least 2 hours or up to 24 hours before serving.

Berry and Beet Salad

Arugula, sometimes referred to as rocket, has a peppery bite that pairs well with the sweet beets and berries. For a milder version, try fresh spinach in place of arugula.

SERVINGS 6 ($^3/_4$ cup each)
CARB. PER SERVING 13 g
START TO FINISH 30 minutes

3 cups chilled roasted* or cooked red and/or orange beets, cubed (about 1$^3/_4$ pounds)

$^1/_4$ cup orange juice

2 tablespoons olive oil

$^1/_4$ teaspoon salt

$^1/_8$ teaspoon black pepper

6 cups fresh arugula

2 cups quartered fresh strawberries

1 ounce goat cheese (chèvre), crumbled

$^1/_4$ cup sliced almonds, toasted

1 Place beets in a medium bowl (reserve liquid that collected while beets were refrigerated). For dressing, in a screw-top jar combine reserved beet juice, orange juice, oil, salt, and pepper. Cover and shake well to combine. Pour dressing over beets.

2 Line a serving platter with the arugula. Top arugula with beet mixture and strawberries; toss to combine. Top with goat cheese and almonds. Serve immediately.

*TEST KITCHEN TIP: To roast beets, preheat oven to 400°F. Wash and trim beets; pat dry with paper towels. Wrap beets in foil. Roast for 1$^1/_4$ to 1$^1/_2$ hours or until tender. Remove from oven; cool slightly. Unwrap beets. While holding a beet under cool running water, slip off and discard skin; repeat with remaining beets. Place beets in a covered container; chill for 1 to 24 hours.

13 grams carb.

PER SERVING: 133 cal., 8 g total fat (2 g sat. fat), 4 mg chol., 165 mg sodium, 13 g carb. (4 g fiber, 8 g sugars), 4 g pro. Exchanges: 2 vegetable, 0.5 fruit, 1.5 fat.

QUICK TIP

Skip roasting and chilling the beets and use two or three 8-ounce packages refrigerated cooked beets instead.

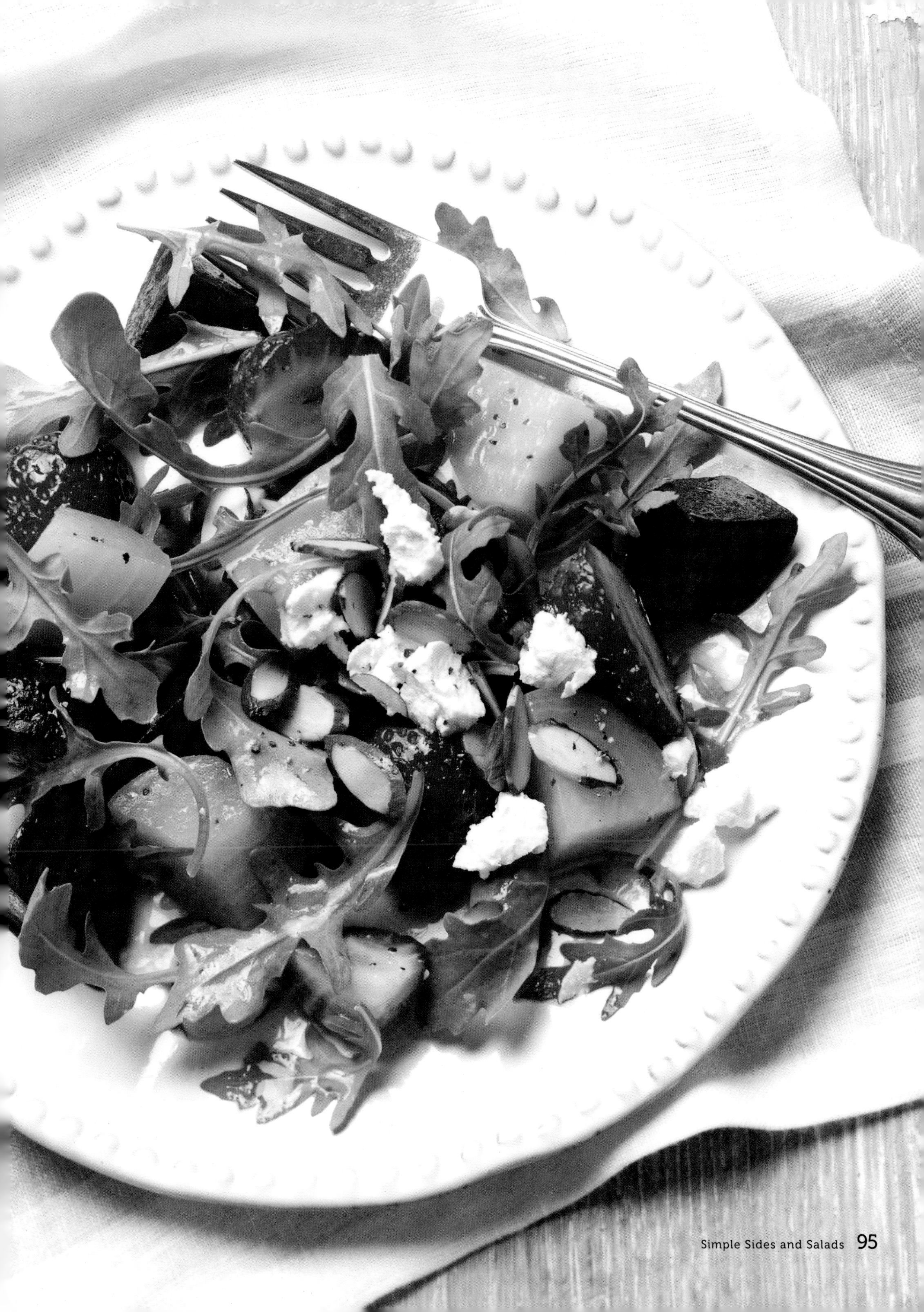

Broccoli and Barley Pilaf

Pistachio nuts add a second touch of green to the mix, but you can substitute chopped roasted almonds if you wish.

SERVINGS 8 ($^1/_2$ cup each)
CARB. PER SERVING 17 g
START TO FINISH 20 minutes

$^2/_3$ cup whole grain (hull-less) barley*

4 cups bite-size pieces fresh broccoli (8 ounces)

2 tablespoons water

3 tablespoons red wine vinegar

2 tablespoons olive oil

1 teaspoon dried Italian seasoning, crushed

$^1/_2$ teaspoon Dijon-style mustard

$^1/_4$ teaspoon salt

1 ripe avocado, halved, seeded, peeled, and coarsely chopped

2 to 3 teaspoons lime juice

2 tablespoons lightly salted pistachio nuts, coarsely chopped

$^1/_4$ cup crumbled reduced-fat feta cheese

PER SERVING: 151 cal., 8 g total fat (1 g sat. fat), 1 mg chol., 146 mg sodium, 17 g carb. (5 g fiber, 1 g sugars), 5 g pro. Exchanges: 1 vegetable, 1 starch, 1.5 fat.

1 | Cook barley according to package directions; drain. Transfer to a large serving bowl; cool to room temperature.

2 | In a microwave-safe dish combine broccoli and the water. Microwave on 100 percent power (high) for 2 to 3 minutes or just until broccoli turns bright green and is slightly tender, stirring once. Drain well. Stir into barley.

3 | For dressing, in a screw-top jar combine vinegar, oil, Italian seasoning, mustard, and salt. Cover and shake well. Toss avocado with the lime juice. Add dressing, avocado, and nuts to the barley-broccoli mixture; gently toss to combine. Serve at room temperature. Sprinkle with feta cheese. Store in the refrigerator.

***TEST KITCHEN TIP:** If you prefer, substitute farro, quinoa, or brown rice for the barley. Start with the dry amount that yields 1$^1/_2$ cups cooked.

Herb and Vegetable Quinoa

Turn this veggie-loaded side dish into a pilaf-style main dish by adding shredded rotisserie chicken.

SERVINGS 8 (1 cup each)
CARB. PER SERVING 19 g
PREP 30 minutes **GRILL** 10 minutes

- ¾ cup quinoa
- ¼ cup red wine vinegar
- 3 tablespoons olive oil
- 2 cloves garlic, minced
- ¼ teaspoon crushed red pepper
- ¼ teaspoon salt
- ¼ teaspoon black pepper
- 1 large red onion (9 ounces), cut into ½-inch-thick rings
- 2 small yellow summer squash (8 ounces each), trimmed and halved lengthwise
- 2 small zucchini (8 ounces each), trimmed and halved lengthwise
- 8 ounces thick fresh asparagus spears, trimmed
- 1 tablespoon snipped fresh thyme
- 1 tablespoons snipped fresh parsley

1 Cook quinoa according to package directions. Drain well in a fine-mesh sieve; keep warm. For vinaigrette, in a screw-top jar combine vinegar, oil, garlic, crushed red pepper, salt, and black pepper. Cover and shake well to combine; set aside.

2 Spread cut vegetables in a single layer on a large baking pan. Brush with 2 tablespoons of the vinaigrette. For a charcoal or gas grill, remove vegetables from baking pan and grill vegetables in a single layer on the rack of a covered grill directly over medium heat for 10 to 12 minutes or until crisp-tender, turning once halfway through grilling time.

3 Transfer grilled vegetables to a cutting board; cut up. Add thyme and parsley to the remaining vinaigrette; cover and shake well. In a large bowl combine cut-up vegetables, cooked quinoa, and herb-vinaigrette mixture.

PER SERVING: 145 cal., 6 g total fat (1 g sat. fat), 0 mg chol., 82 mg sodium, 19 g carb. (3 g fiber, 5 g sugars), 5 g pro. Exchanges: 1 vegetable, 1 starch, 1 fat.

Blueberry Lemon Tabbouleh

To quickly toast the pine nuts, place them in a small skillet and heat and stir over medium heat until lightly golden.

SERVINGS 6 (^{2}/3 cup each)
CARB. PER SERVING 16 g
PREP 25 minutes STAND 10 minutes
CHILL 4 hours

- ½ cup bulgur, rinsed and drained
- ½ cup water
- 1 teaspoon finely shredded lemon peel
- 3 tablespoons lemon juice
- 2 tablespoons olive oil
- 1 teaspoon snipped fresh thyme or lemon thyme
- ½ teaspoon salt
- 1½ cups fresh blueberries
- ½ cup chopped cucumber
- ¼ cup snipped fresh Italian (flat-leaf) parsley
- 2 tablespoons thinly sliced green onion (1)
- 1 cup chopped fresh spinach or watercress leaves
- 2 tablespoons pine nuts, toasted

1 In a small saucepan combine bulgur and the water. Bring to boiling; reduce heat. Simmer, covered, for 5 minutes. Remove from heat; cover and let stand for 10 minutes.

2 Meanwhile, in a medium bowl whisk together lemon peel, lemon juice, oil, thyme, and salt. Add undrained bulgur; toss to coat. Gently stir in blueberries, cucumber, parsley, and green onion. Cover and chill at least 4 hours or up to 24 hours, stirring once or twice.

3 Just before serving, add spinach to bulgur mixture; toss gently to combine. Divide tabbouleh among six serving plates. Sprinkle with pine nuts.

2 grams pro.

PER SERVING: 126 cal., 7 g total fat (1 g sat. fat), 0 mg chol., 203 mg sodium, 16 g carb. (4 g fiber, 4 g sugars), 2 g pro. Exchanges: 0.5 fruit, 0.5 starch, 1.5 fat.

Crumb-Topped Leeks with Mushroom Cream Sauce

Remove and discard the woody stems on the meaty shiitake mushroom caps before finely chopping.

SERVINGS 4 (2 leek halves with crumb topping and 2 tablespoons sauce each)
CARB. PER SERVING 23 g
PREP 25 minutes
BAKE 45 minutes at 350°F

Nonstick cooking spray

4   leeks, trimmed to 4 to 5 inches in length with white and pale green parts

⅓   cup whole wheat panko bread crumbs

⅓   cup snipped fresh Italian (flat-leaf) parsley

3   tablespoons finely shredded Parmesan cheese

3   tablespoons light butter with canola oil, melted

¼   cup finely chopped fresh shiitake mushrooms

2½ teaspoons all-purpose flour

⅛   teaspoon black pepper

½   cup fat-free evaporated milk

PER SERVING: 162 cal., 5 g total fat (2 g sat. fat), 6 mg chol., 199 mg sodium, 23 g carb. (3 g fiber, 8 g sugars), 6 g pro. Exchanges: 2 vegetable, 1 starch, 1 fat.

1 | Preheat oven to 350°F. Coat a 2-quart baking dish with cooking spray. Cut leeks in half lengthwise. Place leek halves, cut sides up, in the prepared baking dish; set aside.

2 | In a small bowl stir together panko, 2 tablespoons of the parsley, the Parmesan cheese, and 2 tablespoons of the melted butter. Sprinkle panko mixture over cut sides of leeks in the baking dish. Cover with foil. Bake for 30 minutes. Uncover; bake about 15 minutes more or until topping is browned and leeks are tender.

3 | Meanwhile, for mushroom sauce, in a small saucepan cook mushrooms in the remaining 1 tablespoon melted butter over medium heat for 3 minutes. Stir in flour and pepper. Add evaporated milk. Cook and stir until thickened and bubbly. Cook and stir for 1 minute more. Stir in the remaining parsley. Divide mushroom sauce among four serving plates. Arrange roasted leeks on top of sauce.

Roasted Cauliflower Steaks

Cut the "steaks" from the center of the cauliflower head, then cut the remaining cauliflower into florets to use for snacking or in another dish.

SERVINGS 6 ($^1/_2$ of a cauliflower steak, $^3/_4$ cup roasted vegetables, and 2 teaspoons Parmesan each)
CARB. PER SERVING 13 g
PREP 30 minutes **ROAST** 25 minutes at 450°F

$^1/_4$ teaspoon crushed red pepper

$2^1/_2$ tablespoons olive oil

1 large head cauliflower ($2^1/_2$ to $2^3/_4$ pounds)

2 10-ounce zucchini, halved lengthwise and cut into $^1/_2$-inch-thick slices (about 5 cups)

2 cups grape tomatoes

1 cup thin wedges red onion

4 cloves garlic, minced

$^1/_4$ teaspoon salt

$^1/_4$ teaspoon freshly ground black pepper

2 tablespoons balsamic vinegar

$^1/_4$ cup shredded Parmesan cheese (1 ounce)

1 Preheat oven to 450°F. In a small bowl stir crushed red pepper into $1^1/_2$ tablespoons of the oil. Brush about one-third of the oil-red pepper mixture onto the bottom of a 3-quart rectangular baking dish.

2 Remove leaves from the cauliflower. Carefully trim stem end, leaving core intact so florets are still attached. Place cauliflower head core side down; cut three 1-inch-thick slices from the center of the cauliflower head. (Refrigerate the remainder of the head for another use.) Place the three cauliflower "steaks" in the prepared baking dish; brush with another third of the oil-red pepper mixture.

3 In another 3-quart rectangular baking dish toss together zucchini, tomatoes, red onion, garlic, salt, black pepper, and the remaining 1 tablespoon olive oil.

4 Place baking dishes side by side in the oven. Roast for 15 minutes. Remove dishes from the oven; carefully turn over cauliflower. Brush with the remaining oil-red pepper mixture. Roast cauliflower for 10 to 15 minutes more or until crisp-tender.

5 Meanwhile, drizzle balsamic vinegar over the zucchini mixture; stir. Roast for 5 to 10 minutes more or until vegetables are crisp-tender and starting to brown.

6 To serve, cut each cauliflower steak in half, cutting through the core so each piece looks like a fan. Spoon the zucchini mixture over cauliflower. Sprinkle with Parmesan cheese.

5 grams pro.

PER SERVING: 133 cal., 8 g total fat (2 g sat. fat), 3 mg chol., 201 mg sodium, 13 g carb. (4 g fiber, 7 g sugars), 5 g pro. Exchanges: 3 vegetable, 1.5 fat.

eye-opening
breakfasts

Start the day right with a good breakfast. Eating well from the

get-go helps you stay on the healthful-eating track all day.

Whether it's a grab-and-run breakfast pudding during the week

or a sit-down egg dish on the weekend, the morning meal gets

you going and sustains you until lunchtime.

Black Bean-Corn Egg Burritos

Wrap up some south-of-the border flavors with these colorful breakfast burritos. They'll keep you fueled all morning.

SERVINGS 6 (1 burrito each)
CARB. PER SERVING 30 g
START TO FINISH 25 minutes

4 eggs

¼ cup milk

¼ teaspoon salt

Dash chili powder

Dash black pepper

⅓ cup chopped green sweet pepper

2 tablespoons snipped fresh cilantro

1 tablespoon olive oil

½ cup canned black beans, rinsed and drained

½ cup whole kernel corn

6 8-inch whole wheat flour tortillas or flour tortillas

Pico de gallo (optional)

½ cup crumbled queso fresco or shredded Monterey Jack cheese (2 ounces)

1 In a small bowl whisk together eggs, milk, salt, chili powder, and black pepper. Stir in sweet pepper and cilantro. In a large skillet heat oil over medium heat; pour in egg mixture. Cook, without stirring, until mixture begins to set on the bottom and around edge. Using a spatula or large spoon, lift and fold the partially cooked egg mixture so the uncooked portion flows underneath. Continue cooking for 2 to 3 minutes more or until egg mixture is cooked through but is still glossy and moist. Remove from heat.

2 In a microwave-safe bowl combine beans and corn. Microwave on 100 percent power (high) for 1 minute, stirring after 30 seconds.

3 Meanwhile, heat tortillas according to package directions. Divide egg mixture among tortillas, spooning it down the centers of the tortillas. Top with black bean-corn mixture. If desired, top with pico de gallo. Sprinkle with cheese. Fold bottom edges of tortillas up and over filling, fold in opposite sides, and roll up from the bottoms. Serve immediately.

PER SERVING: 262 cal., 11 g total fat (4 g sat. fat), 131 mg chol., 578 mg sodium, 30 g carb. (5 g fiber, 4 g sugars), 12 g pro. Exchanges: 2 starch, 1 medium-fat meat, 1 fat.

12 grams pro.

Mini Breakfast Frittatas

Refrigerate leftover frittatas in an airtight container and warm them in the microwave for a quick breakfast to go.

SERVINGS 7 (1 frittata each)
CARB. PER SERVING 5 g
PREP 15 minutes BAKE 20 minutes
at 375°F

Nonstick cooking spray

1½ cups refrigerated or frozen egg product, thawed, or 6 eggs, lightly beaten

6 ounces cooked chicken sausage, chopped

1 cup shredded fresh spinach

¾ cup shredded sharp cheddar cheese (3 ounces)

2 tablespoons finely chopped dried tomatoes (not oil pack)

Sliced green onions (optional)

PER SERVING: 126 cal., 6 g total fat (3 g sat. fat), 30 mg chol., 320 mg sodium, 5 g carb. (0 g fiber, 3 g sugars), 12 g pro. Exchanges: 2 lean meat, 0.5 fat.

1 Preheat oven to 375°F. Coat seven 2½-inch muffin cups with cooking spray; set aside.

2 In a medium bowl combine egg, sausage, spinach, cheese, and tomatoes. Spoon about ⅓ cup of the egg mixture into each prepared muffin cup.

3 Bake for 20 to 25 minutes or until puffed and a knife inserted in the centers comes out clean. Serve immediately. If desired, sprinkle with green onions.

Caprese Egg Crepes

Savory crepes are a light departure from omelets. Fill them with a classic Italian saladlike mixture.

》 SERVINGS 4 (2 egg crepes each)
CARB. PER SERVING 5 g
PREP 20 minutes COOK 10 minutes

2 teaspoons balsamic vinegar

1 teaspoon olive oil

1 cup quartered grape tomatoes

2 ounces fresh mozzarella cheese, cubed, or fresh mozzarella pearls

¼ cup thinly sliced fresh basil

1½ cups refrigerated or frozen egg product, thawed, or 6 eggs, lightly beaten

¼ cup finely chopped onion

¼ cup water

¼ teaspoon black pepper

Nonstick cooking spray

QUICK TIP
Let tomato mixture stand at room temperature for at least 30 minutes for the best flavor and so the crepes stay warm after assembly.

PER SERVING: 107 cal., 4 g total fat (2 g sat. fat), 10 mg chol., 219 mg sodium, 5 g carb. (1 g fiber, 3 g sugars), 12 g pro. Exchanges: 0.5 vegetable, 1.5 lean meat, 0.5 fat.

1 | Preheat oven to 200°F. In a small bowl combine vinegar and oil. Add tomatoes, mozzarella, and basil; toss to coat. Set aside.

2 | In a small bowl whisk together egg, onion, water, and pepper until combined but not frothy. Lightly coat a small nonstick skillet with flared sides with cooking spray. Preheat skillet over medium heat. Add about 3 tablespoons of the egg mixture to skillet. Cook, without stirring, until mixture begins to set on bottom and around edge. Using a spatula, lift and fold the partially cooked egg mixture so the uncooked portion flows underneath. When mixture is set but still shiny and moist, remove skillet from heat. Transfer crepe to a baking sheet; place in oven to keep warm. Repeat to make seven more crepes.

3 | Place 3 tablespoons of the tomato mixture onto one corner of an egg crepe. Fold crepe in quarters. Repeat with remaining crepes and filling. Serve immediately.

Zucchini Patty Egg Stacks

Here's a great use for zucchini! Cook it in patties as a base for this twist on eggs Benedict. Skip the hollandaise and let the yolk act as the sauce.

SERVINGS 4 (1 stack each)
CARB. PER SERVING 6 g
PREP 20 minutes STAND 30 minutes COOK 8 minutes

1½ cups shredded zucchini

⅛ teaspoon salt

1 egg white

2 tablespoons whole grain saltine crackers, crushed

2 tablespoons finely chopped onion

2 tablespoons snipped fresh parsley

1 tablespoon finely shredded Parmesan cheese

⅛ teaspoon black pepper

Nonstick cooking spray

4 teaspoons olive oil

4 slices Canadian-style bacon (2 ounces)

4 cups water

1 tablespoon vinegar

4 eggs

4 teaspoons finely shredded Parmesan cheese

Cracked black pepper (optional)

1 In a medium bowl toss together the zucchini and ⅛ teaspoon salt. Let stand for 30 minutes. Using a clean kitchen towel or double thickness 100-percent-cotton cheesecloth, squeeze out excess water from zucchini (up to 1 cup).

2 In a large bowl whisk egg white until foamy. Stir in zucchini, crackers, onion, parsley, 1 tablespoon Parmesan, and ⅛ teaspoon pepper.

3 Coat a very large nonstick skillet with cooking spray and add olive oil. Heat over medium-high heat. Spoon zucchini mixture into hot oil to form four mounds. Pressing down lightly with the back of a spoon, flatten each mound into a cake about 3 inches in diameter. Cook for 4 to 6 minutes or until golden brown, turning once halfway through cooking. Remove patties from skillet. Keep warm.

4 In the same skillet heat Canadian bacon over medium heat for 1 minute, turning once. Top each zucchini patty with a slice of Canadian bacon. Keep warm.

5 In a large skillet combine water and vinegar. Bring to boiling; reduce heat to simmering. Break an egg into a cup and slip egg into the simmering water. Repeat with remaining eggs, allowing each egg an equal amount of space. Simmer eggs, uncovered, for 3 to 5 minutes or until whites are completely set and yolks begin to thicken but are not hard. Remove eggs from water with a slotted spoon.

6 Transfer eggs to zucchini stacks. Sprinkle stacks with 4 teaspoons Parmesan and, if using, cracked black pepper.

6 grams carb.

PER SERVING: 172 cal., 11 g total fat (3 g sat. fat), 195 mg chol., 396 mg sodium, 6 g carb. (1 g fiber, 2 g sugars), 12 g pro. Exchanges: 0.5 vegetable, 1.5 lean meat, 2 fat.

Moroccan Eggs

Eggs are simmered in a rich, flavorful tomato sauce with chickpeas in this unique breakfast dish.

SERVINGS 4 (1 egg and ³⁄4 cup tomato mixture each)
CARB. PER SERVING 25 g
START TO FINISH 30 minutes

- 1 15-ounce can garbanzo beans (chickpeas), rinsed and drained
- 1 teaspoon paprika
- ½ teaspoon ground cumin
- 2 teaspoons olive oil
- 2 cups low-sodium tomato pasta sauce
- 2 to 3 tablespoons water
- 4 eggs
- ¼ cup snipped fresh cilantro
- 2 tablespoons finely chopped red onion

PER SERVING: 240 cal., 10 g total fat (2 g sat. fat), 189 mg chol., 232 mg sodium, 25 g carb. (3 g fiber, 8 g sugars), 12 g pro. Exchanges: 2 vegetable, 1 starch, 1 medium-fat meat, 1 fat.

1 In a large nonstick skillet cook garbanzo beans, paprika, and cumin in hot oil over medium heat for 10 minutes or until slightly toasted. Stir in pasta sauce and water; heat through. Crack eggs into skillet with sauce. Reduce heat to medium-low. Cover and cook about 8 minutes or until egg whites are set and yolks are desired doneness. To serve, sprinkle with cilantro and onion.

Quick Cornmeal Sausage Pancakes

Pancakes and sausage are a perfect pair. They're even better when you use the sausage to flavor the pancakes.

SERVINGS 1 (2 pancakes each)
CARB. PER SERVING 30 g
START TO FINISH 10 minutes

Nonstick cooking spray

1 link country-style chicken breakfast sausage, such as Al Fresco All Natural brand

1 egg

2 tablespoons cornmeal

1 teaspoon honey

2 tablespoons sugar-free maple-flavor syrup

1 | Lightly coat a small nonstick skillet with cooking spray. Heat over medium-high heat. Using kitchen scissors, snip the sausage link into bite-size pieces over the hot skillet. Cook until browned. Divide sausage into two equal portions.

2 | Meanwhile, in a small bowl whisk together egg, cornmeal, and honey. Pour egg mixture equally over hot sausage portions. Cook for 1 to 2 minutes or until bottoms are set and golden brown. Flip pancakes over and cook for 1 to 2 minutes more or until golden brown. Serve with syrup.

PER SERVING: 234 cal., 8 g total fat (3 g sat. fat), 211 mg chol., 282 mg sodium, 30 g carb. (1 g fiber, 10 g sugars), 14 g pro. Exchanges: 1 starch, 1 carb., 1 lean meat, 1 medium-fat meat.

Overnight Peach-Raspberry French Toast

Wake up and slide these French toast sandwiches in the oven. They're special enough to serve to guests.

SERVINGS 4 (1 French toast sandwich and 2 tablespoons sauce each)
CARB. PER SERVING 49 g or 39 g
PREP 20 minutes **CHILL** overnight **BAKE** 35 minutes at 375°F **STAND** 15 minutes

Nonstick cooking spray

4 ounces fat-free or reduced-fat cream cheese (Neufchâtel), softened

1 fresh peach, finely chopped

8 slices reduced-calorie multigrain bread

1 cup refrigerated or frozen egg product, thawed, or 4 eggs, lightly beaten

1 cup fat-free milk

2 teaspoons granulated sugar*

1 teaspoon vanilla

¼ teaspoon ground cinnamon

1 recipe Raspberry Sauce

1 fresh peach, sliced

1 tablespoon powdered sugar (optional)

1 Coat a 2-quart rectangular baking dish with cooking spray; set aside. In a small bowl stir together cream cheese and chopped peach. Spread mixture evenly on four of the bread slices. Top with the remaining bread slices to make sandwiches. Arrange the four sandwiches in the prepared baking dish.

2 In a medium bowl stir together egg, milk, granulated sugar, vanilla, and cinnamon. Slowly pour egg mixture over sandwiches in baking dish. Use the back of a wide spatula to press the bread into egg mixture to coat. Cover with foil and refrigerate overnight.

3 Preheat oven to 375°F. Bake for 25 minutes. Remove the foil and bake for 10 to 15 minutes more or until the sandwiches puff up and the liquid is absorbed. Remove from oven and place on a wire rack. Let stand for 15 minutes.

4 To serve, place each French toast sandwich on a serving plate. Drizzle with Raspberry Sauce and top with peach slices. If desired, sprinkle with powdered sugar.

RASPBERRY SAUCE: Thaw 2 cups frozen unsweetened raspberries. Do not drain. In a food processor or blender process or blend berries until smooth. Press berries through a fine-mesh sieve; discard seeds. In a small saucepan stir together 3 tablespoons granulated sugar* and 1 teaspoon cornstarch. Add raspberry puree. Cook and stir over medium heat until thickened and bubbly. Cook and stir for 1 minute more. Transfer to a bowl. Serve warm or cover and chill until ready to use.

*SUGAR SUBSTITUTES: Choose from Splenda Granular or Sweet'N Low bulk or packets for the granulated sugar. Follow package directions to use product amounts equivalent to 2 teaspoons granulated sugar and 3 tablespoons granulated sugar.

PER SERVING: 266 cal., 2 g total fat (0 g sat. fat), 5 mg chol., 461 mg sodium, 49 g carb. (11 g fiber, 28 g sugars), 18 g pro. Exchanges: 1 fruit, 1 starch, 1 carb., 2 lean meat.

PER SERVING WITH SUBSTITUTE: Same as above, except 227 cal., 39 g carb. (18 g sugars). Exchanges: 0 carb.

Blueberry Buckwheat Pancakes

Studies have shown that buckwheat may help slow the absorption of glucose after a meal. In pancakes, it's just plain delicious.

SERVINGS 4 (3 pancakes, 1 tablespoon syrup, and 1 teaspoon light butter each)
CARB. PER SERVING 36 g or 35 g
START TO FINISH 30 minutes

½ cup buckwheat flour

½ cup whole wheat flour

1 tablespoon sugar*

½ teaspoon baking powder

½ teaspoon ground cinnamon

¼ teaspoon baking soda

¼ teaspoon salt

¼ cup refrigerated or frozen egg product, thawed, or 1 egg, lightly beaten

1¼ cups buttermilk or sour milk**

1 tablespoon canola oil

½ teaspoon vanilla

¾ cup fresh or frozen blueberries, thawed

¼ cup sugar-free maple-flavor syrup

4 teaspoons light butter with canola oil

PER SERVING: 237 cal., 8 g total fat (2 g sat. fat), 8 mg chol., 450 mg sodium, 36 g carb. (4 g fiber, 10 g sugars), 9 g pro. Exchanges: 2.5 starch, 1 fat.

PER SERVING WITH SUBSTITUTE: Same as above, except 232 cal., 35 g carb. (9 g sugars). Exchanges: 2 starch.

1 | In a medium bowl stir together buckwheat flour, whole wheat flour, sugar, baking powder, cinnamon, baking soda, and salt. Make a well in center of flour mixture; set aside.

2 | In a small bowl combine egg, buttermilk, oil, and vanilla. Add buttermilk mixture all at once to flour mixture. Stir just until combined but still slightly lumpy. Stir in blueberries.

3 | For each pancake, pour about ¼ cup batter onto a hot, lightly greased griddle or heavy skillet. Spread the batter into a circle about 4 inches in diameter. Cook over medium heat for 1 to 2 minutes on each side or until pancakes are golden brown, turning to second sides when pancakes have bubbly surfaces and edges are slightly dry. Serve warm. Top with syrup and butter.

*SUGAR SUBSTITUTES: Choose from Splenda Sugar Blend for Baking or C&H Light Sugar and Stevia Blend. Follow package directions to use product amount equivalent to 1 tablespoon sugar.

**TEST KITCHEN TIP: To make sour milk, place 3¾ teaspoons lemon juice or vinegar in a 2-cup glass measuring cup. Add enough milk to make 1¼ cups total liquid; stir. Let stand 5 minutes before using in the recipe.

Easy Berry Puff Pancake

A heavy cast-iron skillet does the work to make this puff pancake light on the inside but crisp on the outside.

SERVINGS 2 (¹/₂ of a pancake each)
CARB. PER SERVING 29 g
PREP 15 minutes BAKE 10 minutes at 425°F

- 1 egg
- 1 egg white
- ¼ cup flour
- ¼ cup fat-free milk
- 1 tablespoon granulated sugar*
- 1 teaspoon almond extract
- 1 teaspoon finely shredded lemon peel
- 1½ teaspoons butter
- 2 tablespoons sliced almonds
- ²/₃ cup fresh blackberries and/or raspberries
- 2 teaspoons powdered sugar*

PER SERVING: 226 cal., 9 g total fat (3 g sat. fat), 101 mg chol., 102 mg sodium, 29 g carb. (4 g fiber, 13 g sugars), 10 g pro. Exchanges: 1.5 starch, 0.5 carb., 1 lean meat, 1 fat

1 Preheat oven to 425°F. In a medium bowl combine egg, egg white, flour, milk, granulated sugar, almond extract, and lemon peel. Beat with an electric mixer on high speed for 2 minutes.

2 Grease the inside of a 9-inch cast-iron skillet or a dark 9×1½-inch round cake pan with ½ teaspoon of the butter. Place the remaining 1 teaspoon butter in the prepared skillet and put in the hot oven about 2 minutes or until butter is melted and starting to sizzle.

3 Pour batter into the hot skillet or pan; quickly sprinkle with almonds. Bake for 10 to 12 minutes or until mixture puffs in center and browns and crisps on edges. Immediately remove pancake from skillet or pan and place on a cooling rack to prevent the bottom from becoming soggy. Cool slightly. Top with berries. Sift powdered sugar over all.

*SUGAR SUBSTITUTES: We do not recommend using a sugar substitute for this recipe.

Pumpkin-Walnut Baked French Toast with Maple-Coffee Syrup

If you like coffee in the morning, you'll love the hint of coffee in the syrup for this French toast.

SERVINGS 8 (1 piece French toast and about 2 tablespoons syrup each)
CARB. PER SERVING 31 g
PREP 25 minutes CHILL 2 hours BAKE 25 minutes at 350°F COOK 5 minutes

Nonstick cooking spray

- 6 cups cubed and dried reduced calorie wheat bread (8 ounces)
- 1½ cups fat-free milk
- 1¼ cups refrigerated or frozen egg product, thawed, or 3 eggs, lightly beaten
- ¾ cup canned pumpkin
- ¼ cup packed brown sugar*
- 1 teaspoon ground cinnamon
- ¼ teaspoon ground nutmeg
- 1 cup chopped walnuts, toasted
- 2 tablespoons granulated sugar*
- 1 tablespoon cornstarch
- ⅔ cup water
- 1 teaspoon instant coffee crystals
- ⅓ cup reduced-calorie maple-flavor syrup
- ½ teaspoon vanilla

Banana slices (optional)

1 Coat a 3-quart rectangular baking dish with cooking spray. Arrange the dried bread cubes in the prepared baking dish.

2 In a large bowl whisk together milk, egg, pumpkin, brown sugar, cinnamon, and nutmeg until smooth. Gradually pour egg mixture over bread; press lightly with the back of a large spoon to moisten bread. Sprinkle walnuts evenly over bread. Cover and chill for 2 to 24 hours.

3 Preheat oven to 350°F. Bake, uncovered, for 25 to 30 minutes or until a toothpick inserted in center comes out clean. Let stand 10 minutes before serving.

4 For maple-coffee syrup, in a small saucepan combine granulated sugar and cornstarch. Whisk in water. Cook and stir over medium heat until thickened and bubbly. Cook and stir for 2 minutes more. Remove from heat and stir in instant coffee crystals, syrup, and vanilla.

5 Cut French toast into eight pieces and divide among serving plates. If desired, garnish each serving with banana slices. Drizzle with warm syrup and serve warm.

*SUGAR SUBSTITUTES: We do not recommend using sugar substitutes for this recipe.

PER SERVING: 257 cal., 10 g total fat (1 g sat. fat), 1 mg chol., 230 mg sodium, 31 g carb. (5 g fiber, 19 g sugars), 12 g pro. Exchanges: 1 starch, 1 carb., 1.5 lean meat, 1.5 fat.

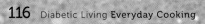

Honey-Almond Breakfast Biscuits with Mango-Apricot Spread

Ground almonds and almond flour are unexpected ingredients that add a nutty flavor and chewy texture to these biscuits.

SERVINGS 25 (1 biscuit with 1 teaspoon spread each)
CARB. PER SERVING 17 g
PREP 25 minutes **BAKE** 10 minutes at 400°F **MICROWAVE** 1 minute

2²⁄₃ cups all-purpose flour

²⁄₃ cup whole wheat pastry flour

¼ cup almond flour

¼ cup finely chopped, toasted almonds

1 tablespoon baking powder

¼ teaspoon salt

¹⁄₃ cup cold light butter, cut up

²⁄₃ cup fat-free milk

½ cup refrigerated or frozen egg product, thawed, or 2 eggs, lightly beaten

¼ cup honey

½ cup chopped refrigerated mango slices

¹⁄₃ cup low-sugar apricot preserves

¹⁄₈ teaspoon ground cardamom

1 Preheat oven to 400°F. In a large bowl combine flours, almonds, baking powder, and salt. Using a pastry blender, cut in light butter until mixture resembles coarse crumbs. Make a well in center of the flour mixture; set mixture aside.

2 In a medium bowl combine milk, eggs, and honey. Add milk mixture all at once to flour mixture. Using a fork, stir just until moistened.

3 Turn dough out onto a floured surface. Knead dough by folding and gently pressing it 6 to 8 strokes or until dough is nearly smooth. Pat or lightly roll dough to ³⁄₄-inch thickness. Using a 2-inch fluted round cutter, cut out biscuits. Reroll scraps as needed; avoid overworking the dough when rerolling to prevent tough biscuits. Place dough circles 2 inches apart on a very large greased baking sheet.

4 Bake about 10 minutes or until golden brown. Cool slightly on a wire rack.

5 For the spread, place mango in a small microwave-safe bowl. Cover with vented plastic wrap. Microwave on 100 percent power (high) for 1 to 1½ minutes or until mango is tender, stirring once. Mash with a fork or potato masher. Stir in apricot preserves and cardamom. Serve with warm biscuits.

PER SERVING: 99 cal., 2 g total fat (1 g sat. fat), 3 mg chol., 116 mg sodium, 17 g carb. (1 g fiber, 5 g sugars), 3 g pro. Exchanges: 1 starch, 0.5 fat.

2 grams fat

Tropical Fruit Breakfast Parfaits

These colorful parfaits make a pretty addition to a brunch buffet. They can just as easily head out the door with you in a travel container.

SERVINGS 8 (1 parfait each)
CARB. PER SERVING 23 g or 22 g
PREP 20 minutes BAKE 20 minutes at 350°F CHILL 4 hours

Nonstick cooking spray

4 cups regular rolled oats

1/3 cup shredded coconut

1/2 cup dry-roasted unsalted sunflower kernels

1/4 cup honey

3 tablespoons canola oil

2 tablespoons packed brown sugar*

2 1/2 cups cubed tropical fruits, such as mangoes, kiwifruits, papayas, bananas, and/or pineapple

2 cups coconut- or honey-flavor Greek yogurt

Toasted shredded coconut (optional)

Chopped macadamia nuts (optional)

1 For granola, preheat oven to 350°F. Lightly coat a 15×10×1-inch baking pan with cooking spray; set aside. In a medium bowl combine oats, the 1/3 cup coconut, and the sunflower kernels. In a small bowl combine honey, oil, and brown sugar. Drizzle honey mixture over oat mixture. Stir until oats are coated. Spread evenly in prepared pan.

2 Bake for 20 to 25 minutes or until lightly browned, stirring twice. Line a large baking sheet with foil or parchment paper. Spread granola onto prepared baking sheet; cool. Store in an airtight container at room temperature up to 1 week. (You will have more granola than you need to make the parfaits. Use the extra as a topping for ice cream or pudding or to add crunch to salads or a peanut butter sandwich.)

3 To make parfaits, place about 2 tablespoons of the cubed fruit in each of eight 6- to 8-ounce glasses. Add about 2 tablespoons of the yogurt to each glass. Add about 1 tablespoon of the granola to each glass. Repeat layers once more. Do not stir. If desired, top with toasted coconut and macadamia nuts. Serve immediately or cover and chill up to 4 hours.

*SUGAR SUBSTITUTE: Choose Splenda Brown Sugar Blend for Baking. Follow package directions to use product amount equivalent to 2 tablespoons brown sugar.

PEACH BREAKFAST PARFAITS: Prepare granola as directed, except stir 1 teaspoon ground cinnamon into honey mixture. Assemble parfaits as directed, except substitute chopped, peeled peaches for the tropical fruits and use peach- or honey-flavor Greek yogurt. If desired, garnish with sliced peaches and purchased glazed almonds or walnuts.

PER SERVING: 155 cal., 5 g total fat (2 g sat. fat), 8 mg chol., 33 mg sodium, 23 g carb. (2 g fiber, 14 g sugars), 8 g pro. Exchanges: 0.5 milk, 0.5 fruit, 0.5 starch, 0.5 lean meat, 0.5 fat.

PER SERVING WITH SUBSTITUTE: Same as above, except 154 cal., 22 g carb.

PER SERVING PEACH VERSION: 120 cal., 2 g total fat (0 g sat. fat), 0 mg chol., 25 mg sodium, 19 g carb. (2 g fiber, 13 g sugars), 7 g pro. Exchanges: 0.5 milk, 0.5 fruit, 0.5 starch.

PER SERVING PEACH VERSION WITH SUBSTITUTE: Same as above, except 119 cal.

To toast coconut, spread it evenly in a shallow pan. Bake in a 350°F oven for 5 to 10 minutes, shaking the pan once or twice and watching carefully so it doesn't burn.

Cherry-Blueberry Banana Smoothies

Frozen fruit makes a thicker smoothie. You can use all fresh fruit, but you may want to add some ice cubes to the blender to make the drink thicker.

SERVINGS 4 (^{3}/4 cup each)
CARB. PER SERVING 20 g
START TO FINISH 10 minutes

1½ cups frozen unsweetened pitted dark sweet cherries or sour cherries

1 cup unsweetened vanilla-flavor almond milk

1 6-ounce carton blueberry-flavor fat-free Greek yogurt

½ cup fresh or frozen unsweetened blueberries

1 small banana, peeled

1 In a blender combine cherries, almond milk, yogurt, blueberries, and banana. Cover and blend until smooth. Pour into glasses to serve.

PER SERVING: 104 cal., 1 g total fat (0 g sat. fat), 0 mg chol., 62 mg sodium, 20 g carb. (3 g fiber, 16 g sugars), 5 g pro. Exchanges: 0.5 milk, 1 fruit.

Chia Pudding with Fruit

Step aside, tapioca. Chia seeds bring their thickening power to this pudding. It will keep you satisfied without weighing you down.

SERVINGS 6 (¹/₂ cup pudding and ¹/₃ cup fruit each)
CARB. PER SERVING 18 g
PREP 20 minutes   **CHILL** overnight

- 1   14-ounce can unsweetened light coconut milk
- 1   cup plain fat-free Greek yogurt
- 2   tablespoons pure maple syrup
- ¹/₂   teaspoon vanilla
- ¹/₄   cup chia seeds
- 2   cups chopped fresh fruit or berries, such as pineapple, strawberries, blueberries, raspberries, mango, and/or peach
- 6   teaspoons unsweetened shredded coconut, toasted

PER SERVING: 161 cal., 8 g total fat (4 g sat. fat), 0 mg chol., 30 mg sodium, 18 g carb. (4 g fiber, 12 g sugars), 7 g pro. Exchanges: 0.5 fruit, 0.5 starch, 1 lean meat, 1 fat.

1 In medium bowl stir together the coconut milk, yogurt, maple syrup, and vanilla. Stir in the chia seeds. Divide mixture among four serving bowls. Cover; chill overnight.

2 To serve, spoon fruit evenly over pudding in bowls. Sprinkle with coconut.

QUICK TIP
Chia seeds are high in omega-3 fatty acids, protein, and fiber. They expand when mixed with liquid, and this helps you feel full longer.

7

good-for-you
snacks

A healthful way to keep your stomach from rumbling and your

blood sugars from spiking is to eat a snack between meals. Like

meals, snacks offering a combo of carbohydrate, fat, and protein

are best. Turn the page to discover delicious new snack recipes.

Cheddar and Apple Wafflewiches

A toasted whole grain waffle serves as the bread in this sandwichlike snack. When pears are in their prime, use one instead of apple.

SERVINGS 2 (1 wafflewich half each)
CARB. PER SERVING 17 g
START TO FINISH 10 minutes

2 frozen whole grain waffles

1 teaspoon Dijon-style mustard

8 thin slices tart apple

1 ultrathin slice cheddar or Swiss cheese

1 | Toast waffles according to package directions. Spread mustard on one waffle. Top with apple slices, cheese, and second waffle. Cut wafflewich in half to serve.

17 grams carb.

PER SERVING: 124 cal., 5 g total fat (2 g sat. fat), 5 mg chol., 293 mg sodium, 17 g carb. (2 g fiber, 5 g sugars), 4 g pro. Exchanges: 1 starch, 1 fat.

Carrot-Mango Green Tea Smoothies

Budget-friendly tip: Buy fresh mangoes during peak season and peel, seed, and cut into chunks. Store the fruit chunks in a freezer bag in the freezer.

SERVINGS 4 ($^3/_4$ cup each)
CARB. PER SERVING 21 g
PREP 10 minutes **COOK** 10 minutes
STAND 2 minutes **CHILL** 10 minutes

3 cups water

1 cup sliced carrots

1 inch fresh ginger, thinly sliced

4 green tea bags

2 cups frozen mango chunks

1 teaspoon honey

1 tablespoon chia seeds (optional)

PER SERVING: 80 cal., 0 g total fat, 0 mg chol., 28 mg sodium, 21 g carb. (1 g fiber, 17 g sugars), 1 g pro. Exchanges: 0.5 vegetable, 1 fruit.

1 In a small saucepan bring water to boiling. Add carrots; cover and cook for 10 to 15 minutes or until very tender, adding ginger slices the last 2 minutes of cooking. Remove from heat and add tea bags. Cover and steep for 2 minutes.

2 Remove tea bags, squeezing out all the tea; discard bags. Remove and discard ginger slices. Set pan on a hot pad in the refrigerator for 10 minutes. Transfer carrot-tea mixture to a blender. Add mango, honey, and chia seeds (if using). Cover and blend until smooth. Pour into four glasses to serve.

Greek Cucumber Boats

Go with the common cucumber rather than the slender English variety for making these fresh and tasty handheld snacks.

SERVINGS 4 (1 filled cucumber quarter each)
CARB. PER SERVING 10 g
START TO FINISH 10 minutes

- 1   large cucumber
- ½ to ¾ cup purchased plain or roasted red pepper hummus
- ¼   cup quartered grape or cherry tomatoes
- 2   tablespoons reduced-fat feta cheese
- 2   teaspoons snipped fresh dill weed or oregano

PER SERVING: 80 cal., 3 g total fat (1 g sat. fat), 1 mg chol., 136 mg sodium, 10 g carb. (2 g fiber, 2 g sugars), 3 g pro. Exchanges: 0.5 vegetable, 0.5 starch, 0.5 fat.

PER SERVING PEPPERONCINI VERSION: Same as above, except 81 cal., 11 g carb., 142 mg sodium.

1 | Cut cucumber in half lengthwise. Cut each half in half crosswise. Using a mellon baller or small spoon, slightly hollow out the cucumber quarters by scooping out the seeds. Spoon 2 to 3 tablespoons hummus evenly into each cucumber quarter. Sprinkle tomatoes, feta, and dill evenly over hummus.

PEPPERONCINI CUCUMBER BOATS: Prepare as directed, except omit the dill. Top each cucumber quarter with 2 or 3 pepperoncini slices in addition to the tomato and feta. Sprinkle with 2 teaspoons snipped fresh oregano.

Banh Mi Lettuce Wraps

Some romaine leaves are quite large. Trim the leaves as necessary to create small lettuce cups.

SERVINGS 4 (1 wrap each)
CARB. PER SERVING 3 g
START TO FINISH 10 minutes

- ⅓ cup shredded carrot
- ⅓ cup shredded daikon radish
- ¼ of a medium cucumber, cut into matchstick-size pieces
- 1 tablespoon snipped fresh cilantro
- 2 teaspoons rice wine vinegar
- 2 teaspoons reduced-sodium soy sauce
- 1 cup shredded cooked chicken breast
- 4 small romaine leaves

PER SERVING: 70 cal., 1 g total fat (0 g sat. fat), 30 mg chol., 132 mg sodium, 3 g carb. (1 g fiber, 1 g sugars), 11 g pro. Exchanges: 0.5 vegetable, 1.5 lean meat.

1 In a small bowl stir together carrot, radish, cucumber, cilantro, vinegar, and soy sauce. Divide chicken among lettuce leaves. Using a slotted spoon, top with carrot mixture.

QUICK TIP
Take this hearty snack to the lunch level and serve two people.

Trees and Raisins Crackers

The ingredients found in the popular potluck salad top these crisp crackers, so you get the same great flavor.

SERVINGS 4 (2 crackers each)
CARB. PER SERVING 19 g
START TO FINISH 25 minutes

- ½ cup light cream cheese spread, softened
- 2 tablespoons finely chopped red onion
- 2 teaspoons snipped fresh parsley
- ⅛ teaspoon black pepper
- 8 3½x1½-inch crisp rye crackers
- ¾ cup chopped broccoli
- 2 tablespoons snipped golden raisins or dried cranberries
- 1 tablespoon sunflower kernels

PER SERVING: 155 cal., 7 g total fat (3 g sat. fat), 20 mg chol., 237 mg sodium, 19 g carb. (4 g fiber, 6 g sugars), 4 g pro. Exchanges: 1 starch, 1 fat.

1 In a small bowl stir together cream cheese, onion, parsley, and pepper. Spread evenly on crackers. Top evenly with broccoli, raisins, and sunflower kernels.

Caramel Cheese Crazy Corn

Measure out each serving of this crunchy treat—once you start eating this colorful mix, it's hard to stop.

SERVINGS 10 (2$\frac{1}{2}$ cups each)
CARB. PER SERVING 24 g
PREP 45 minutes **BAKE** 1 hour

Nonstick cooking spray

25 cups popped butter-flavor 94% fat-free microwave popcorn (2 to 3 bags)

5 tablespoons butter

$\frac{1}{2}$ cup packed brown sugar*

2 tablespoons honey

$\frac{1}{2}$ teaspoon vanilla

$\frac{1}{8}$ teaspoon baking soda

1 teaspoon ground turmeric

3 tablespoons grated Parmesan cheese

1 Coat two large baking dishes with cooking spray; set aside. Preheat oven to 250°F. Place 7 cups of the popped corn in a very large bowl or roasting pan; set aside. Place 9 cups of the remaining popped corn in each of two very large bowls.

2 For caramel, in a heavy medium saucepan melt 3 tablespoons of the butter over medium heat. Stir in brown sugar and honey. Cook and stir until boiling. Reduce heat slightly but continue to allow mixture to boil at a moderate, steady rate, without stirring, for 3 minutes. Remove saucepan from heat; stir in vanilla and baking soda. Slowly pour caramel over 9 cups of the popped corn in one of the bowls. Stir gently to coat. Transfer mixture to one of the prepared baking dishes.

3 In a small heavy saucepan melt the remaining 2 tablespoons butter over medium heat. When melted, stir in the turmeric until dissolved. Pour butter mixture over the 9 cups popped corn in the other bowl; toss gently so popcorn becomes evenly yellow. Sprinkle with Parmesan cheese; toss to coat. Transfer mixture to the remaining prepared baking dish, scraping bowl well.

4 Bake mixtures in both baking dishes for 15 minutes. Gently stir. Repeat baking and stirring three times for the caramel corn and twice for the cheese corn or until each popcorn mix is crisp.

5 Remove popcorn from oven. Spread popcorn on large pieces of waxed paper; cool. When completely cooled, add the caramel corn and cheese corn to the reserved plain popcorn in the very large bowl or roasting pan; stir to mix well.

6 Package in 2$\frac{1}{2}$-cup portions. Store at room temperature for up to 3 days.

*SUGAR SUBSTITUTE: We do not recommend using a sugar substitute for this recipe.

PER SERVING: 166 cal., 6 g total fat (4 g sat. fat), 18 mg chol., 221 mg sodium, 24 g carb. (1 g fiber, 14 g sugars), 2 g pro. Exchanges: 0.5 starch, 1 carb., 1 fat.

Chocolate Peanut Butter Cookie Dough Dip

Rather than eating raw cookie dough, play it safe with this delicious dip. You'll get yummy cookie flavor with no baking involved!

SERVINGS 18 (2 tablespoons dip and 2 graham crackers each)
CARB. PER SERVING 24 g
PREP 15 minutes   **COOK** 5 minutes   **STAND** 5 minutes

½ cup water

¼ cup pitted dates

1 15-ounce can no-salt-added cannellini beans, rinsed and drained

½ cup creamy peanut butter

1 teaspoon vanilla

⅛ teaspoon salt

½ cup dark chocolate pieces

¼ cup quick-cooking rolled oats

36 low-fat graham cracker squares

1 In a small saucepan bring water and dates to boiling; reduce heat. Simmer, covered, about 5 minutes or until dates are very soft. Remove from heat and cool.

2 Transfer dates and cooking liquid to a food processor. Add beans, peanut butter, vanilla, and salt. Cover and process until smooth, scraping sides of bowl occasionally.

3 Transfer bean mixture to a medium bowl and stir in chocolate pieces and oats. Cover and let stand 5 minutes before serving. Serve with graham crackers for dipping.

*TEST KITCHEN TIP: Store dip in an airtight container in the refrigerator for up to 3 days or freeze for up to 6 months.

PER SERVING: 167 cal., 6 g total fat (2 g sat. fat), 0 mg chol., 167 mg sodium, 24 g carb. (2 g fiber, 9 g sugars), 4 g pro. Exchanges: 1.5 starch, 1 fat.

4 grams pro.

QUICK TIP
This party-perfect dip makes 2¼ cups. Or place the dip in small freezer containers or bags and freeze for up to 6 month. You can have your cookie dough fix whenever you get the craving!

PB and Jelly Poppers

Bring the kids into the kitchen to help assemble these yummy bites. Let them pick their favorite flavor of preserves.

SERVINGS 4 (3 poppers each)
CARB. PER SERVING 13 g
START TO FINISH 15 minutes

- ⅓ cup light cream cheese spread, softened
- 1 tablespoon powdered peanut butter
- ¼ teaspoon ground ginger or apple pie spice
- 12 miniature caramel corn- or apple-cinnamon-flavor rice cakes
- ¼ cup desired-flavor sugar-free preserves
- 2 tablespoons miniature semisweet chocolate pieces (optional)

QUICK TIP
Keep a bowl of the cream cheese-peanut butter mixture stirred together in the fridge to have on hand when you need a snack.

PER SERVING: 88 cal., 4 g total fat (2 g sat. fat), 13 mg chol., 170 mg sodium, 13 g carb. (0 g fiber, 3 g sugars), 2 g pro. Exchanges: 1 starch, 0.5 fat.

1 | In a small bowl stir together cream cheese, peanut butter, and ginger. Spread evenly on rice cakes. Top with preserves. If desired, sprinkle with chocolate pieces.

Carrot Cake Yogurt

Transform plain Greek yogurt into a naturally sweet delight.
Each bite is reminiscent of the beloved carrot cake.

SERVINGS 4 (1/3 cup each)
CARB. PER SERVING 14 g
START TO FINISH 15 minutes

1½ cups plain fat-free Greek yogurt

½ cup finely shredded carrot

¼ cup reduced-fat cream cheese
(Neufchâtel), softened

1 tablespoon pure maple syrup

½ teaspoon finely shredded
orange peel

⅛ teaspoon ground cinnamon

2 tablespoons chopped walnuts,
toasted

2 tablespoons unsweetened
shredded coconut, toasted

4 teaspoons pure maple syrup

PER SERVING: 141 cal., 5 g total fat
(2 g sat. fat), 5 mg chol.,
69 mg sodium, 14 g carb. (1 g fiber,
12 g sugars), 10 g pro. Exchanges:
0.5 starch, 0.5 carb., 1 lean meat,
0.5 fat.

1 In a medium bowl beat together the yogurt, carrot, cream cheese, maple syrup, orange peel, and cinnamon with an electric mixer.

2 Divide among four small serving dishes. Top evenly with walnuts and coconut. Drizzle each dish with 1 teaspoon pure maple syrup before serving.

Mango Gazpacho Parfaits

There's a cool burst of freshness with each bite of this tropical fruit and yogurt treat.

SERVINGS 4 (1 parfait each)
CARB. PER SERVING 15 g
START TO FINISH 15 minutes

1 cup chopped fresh mango or refrigerated mango slices

1 cup chopped fresh pineapple

½ cup finely chopped red sweet pepper

1 tablespoon orange juice

1 teaspoon finely shredded lime peel

1 tablespoon snipped fresh cilantro

⅛ teaspoon salt

⅛ to ¼ teaspoon crushed red pepper

1 cup plain fat-free Greek yogurt

1 In a medium bowl stir together the mango, pineapple, sweet pepper, orange juice, lime peel, snipped cilantro, salt, and crushed red pepper.

2 Divide half of the yogurt among four glasses or parfait glasses. Top with half of the mango mixture. Repeat layers with the remaining yogurt and mango mixture.

PER SERVING: 85 cal., 0 g total fat, 0 mg chol., 96 mg sodium, 15 g carb. (2 g fiber, 13 g sugars), 7 g pro. Exchanges: 1 fruit, 1 lean meat.

7 grams pro.

QUICK TIP
The mango and pineapple mixture gets juicy, so prepare the parfaits just before serving.

Chia Granola Clusters

Gently squeeze the oaty mixture together to form the clusters.

>> SERVINGS 12 (¹/₃ cup each)
CARB. PER SERVING 23 g
PREP 35 minutes   STAND 15 minutes
BAKE 1 hour

- ³/₄ cup unsweetened applesauce
- ¹/₄ cup pure maple syrup
- 2 tablespoons chia seeds
- 4 teaspoons canola oil
- 2 teaspoons vanilla
- ¹/₂ teaspoon ground cinnamon
- ¹/₄ teaspoon salt
- ¹/₄ teaspoon ground ginger
- 3 cups regular rolled oats
- ¹/₄ cup chopped almonds
- 2 tablespoons flaxseed meal
- 2 tablespoons wheat germ

PER SERVING: 161 cal., 6 g total fat (1 g sat. fat), 0 mg chol., 51 mg sodium, 23 g carb. (5 g fiber, 7 g sugars), 4 g pro. Exchanges: 1.5 starch, 1 fat.

1 Preheat oven to 300°F. Line a 15x10x1-inch baking pan with foil; set aside. In a small bowl stir together the applesauce, maple syrup, chia seeds, canola oil, vanilla, cinnamon, salt, and ginger. Let stand for 15 minutes.

2 In a medium bowl stir together the oats, almonds, flaxseed meal, and wheat germ. Stir in the applesauce mixture until combined. For each cluster, pinch and squeeze about 1 teaspoon of the mixture together. Place clusters in a single layer in the prepared baking pan.

3 Bake for 30 minutes; stir gently. Continue baking about 30 minutes or until light golden, gently stirring every 15 minutes. Cool completely in pan on a wire rack. Store in an airtight container up to 5 days or freeze up to 2 months.

Strawberry-Lime Coolers

Pour this bubbly beverage over ice to serve.

>> SERVINGS 8 (scant 1 cup cooler plus ice each)
CARB. PER SERVING 16 g
START TO FINISH 15 minutes

- 4 cups fresh strawberries, cut up
- 2 cups coconut water
- 3 tablespoons honey
- 2 tablespoons lime juice
- 2 cups club soda

1 In a blender combine strawberries, coconut water, honey, and lime juice. Cover and blend until smooth. Stir in club soda. Pour over *ice* to serve. Garnish with *lime slices*.

0 gram fat

PER SERVING: 60 cal., 0 g total fat, 0 mg chol., 17 mg sodium, 16 g carb. (2 g fiber, 12 g sugars), 1 g pro. Exchanges: 0.5 fruit, 0.5 carb.

delightful
desserts

Whether it's studded with chocolate or crowned with fruit,

a little something sweet always puts a special ending on an

everyday meal. Keep a tally of carbohydrates you consume

throughout the day to ensure there's room in your meal plan

for a delicious dessert.

Mint Cream-Filled Chocolate Cupcakes

A bit of melted chocolate seals the hole where the filling is piped in, then dries to afix the candy topping.

SERVINGS 24 (1 cupcake each)
CARB. PER SERVING 28 g or 22 g
PREP 35 minutes **BAKE** 15 minutes at 350°F
COOL 5 minutes **STAND** 30 minutes

2 cups all-purpose flour

$3/4$ cup unsweetened cocoa powder

$1^1/2$ teaspoons baking soda

$1/2$ teaspoon salt

$1^1/3$ cups sugar*

$1/3$ cup canola oil

$3/4$ cup refrigerated or frozen egg product, thawed

$1/2$ teaspoon vanilla

$1/2$ teaspoon peppermint extract

$1^1/2$ cups buttermilk

1 teaspoon peppermint extract

Green food coloring

$1/2$ of an 8-ounce container frozen light whipped dessert topping, thawed

$1/2$ cup semisweet chocolate pieces

1 teaspoon shortening

24 miniature chocolate-covered mint cream candies, such as Junior Mints brand, or 12 layered chocolate mint candies, such as Andes brand, halved

PER SERVING: 167 cal., 6 g total fat (2 g sat. fat), 1 mg chol., 161 mg sodium, 28 g carb. (1 g fiber, 17 g sugars), 3 g pro. Exchanges: 1 starch, 1 carb., 1 fat.

PER SERVING WITH SUBSTITUTE: Same as above, except 150 cal., 22 g carb. (11 g sugars). Exchanges: 0.5 carb.

1 Preheat oven to 350°F. Line twenty-four $2^1/2$-inch muffin cups with foil bake cups; set aside.

2 In a medium bowl combine flour, cocoa powder, baking soda, and salt. In a large bowl combine sugar and oil; beat with an electric mixer on medium to high speed until combined. Add egg, vanilla, and the $1/2$ teaspoon peppermint extract, beating until combined. Alternately add flour mixture and buttermilk to beaten mixture, beating on low speed after each addition until combined.

3 Divide batter among prepared muffin cups, filling each cup about half full. Bake about 15 minutes or until tops of cupcakes spring back when lightly touched. Cool for 5 minutes in muffin cups on a wire rack. Remove from muffin cups; cool completely.

4 In a medium bowl fold 1 teaspoon peppermint extract and about 12 drops green food coloring into the whipped topping. Transfer topping to a pastry bag fitted with a small round tip. Using a straw, poke a hole in the center of each cooled cupcake, pushing halfway into the cupcake. Insert tip of pastry bag into each hole and squeeze to fill each with filling (stop squeezing when you see the filling coming out of the hole).

5 In a small microwave-safe bowl combine chocolate pieces and shortening. Microwave on 100 percent power (high) about 30 seconds or until melted and smooth, stirring every 10 seconds. Spoon or pipe a button of chocolate in the center of each cupcake, covering the hole in center. Place a mint candy piece in the chocolate on each cupcake. Let stand about 30 minutes or until chocolate sets. (For an attractive presentation, use foil bake cups and place each baked cupcake inside a decorative paper bake cup.)

*****SUGAR SUBSTITUTE:** Choose Splenda Sugar Blend for Baking. Follow package directions to use product amount equivalent to $1^1/3$ cups sugar.

Chocolate Chip Almond Biscotti

Store these crunchy cookies in an airtight container at room temperature for up to 3 days or in a freezer container in the freezer for up to 3 months.

SERVINGS 30 (1 biscotti each)
CARB. PER SERVING 13 g
PREP 30 minutes **BAKE** 45 minutes at 325°F

⅛ teaspoon canola oil

1¼ cups whole wheat flour

½ cup all-purpose flour

½ cup sugar*

1 teaspoon baking powder

½ teaspoon salt

¾ cup miniature semisweet chocolate pieces

½ cup chopped or sliced almonds

½ cup refrigerated or frozen egg product, thawed

2 tablespoons butter, melted

1 teaspoon almond extract

1 Preheat oven to 325°F. Lightly grease a large cookie sheet with the canola oil; set aside. In a large bowl combine flours, sugar, baking powder, and salt. Stir in chocolate pieces and almonds. Make a well in the center of the flour mixture; set aside.

2 In a small bowl whisk together egg, butter, and almond extract. Pour egg mixture into the well in flour mixture; stir to combine. Using your hands, gently knead dough until it comes together. Divide the dough in half.

3 On a lightly floured surface, roll each dough half into a 10-inch-long log. Place logs on prepared cookie sheet about 3 inches apart. Flatten each log so it is about 2 inches wide; press in short ends to make even. Bake for 25 to 30 minutes or until firm and lightly browned.

4 Cool completely on the baking sheet. Transfer to a cutting board. Using a serrated knife, cut each log diagonally into 15 slices, each about ½ inch thick. Place slices, cut sides down, on the same cookie sheet. Bake in the 325°F oven for 10 minutes. Turn slices over. Bake for 10 minutes more. Transfer to a wire rack; cool completely.

*SUGAR SUBSTITUTES: We do not recommend using a sugar substitute for this recipe.

PER SERVING: 84 cal., 3 g total fat (2 g sat. fat), 2 mg chol., 70 mg sodium, 13 g carb. (1 g fiber, 7 g sugars), 2 g pro. Exchanges: 1 starch, 0.5 fat.

Walnut-Apricot Baklava Bites

The tiny pastry shells are often found in the freezer section, but during the holiday season you may find them in a special display.

SERVINGS 15 (2 tarts each)
CARB. PER SERVING 12 g
START TO FINISH 10 minutes

- 1 cup chopped toasted walnuts
- 6 tablespoons chopped dried apricots
- 4 teaspoons finely chopped crystallized ginger
- 2 2.1-ounce packages baked miniature phyllo tart shells (30)
- ¼ cup honey
- ¼ teaspoon ground nutmeg

PER SERVING: 107 cal., 6 g total fat (0 g sat. fat), 0 mg chol., 26 mg sodium, 12 g carb. (1 g fiber, 6 g sugars), 2 g pro. Exchanges: 1 starch, 1 fat.

1 In a small bowl stir together walnuts, apricots, and ginger. Spoon evenly into tart shells. Drizzle with honey and sprinkle with nutmeg. Serve immediately.

MAKE-AHEAD DIRECTIONS: Place tarts in a single layer in an airtight container; cover. Store in the refrigerator for up to 48 hours.

QUICK TIP

Use the recipe as a guide and adapt the fruits and nuts to your liking. Try toasted almonds or pecans for the walnuts and sub dried cranberries or cherries for some of the dried apricots.

Vanilla Pudding Pops with Strawberry-Basil Ribbon

If you have eight plastic frozen pop molds, use them instead of the 5-ounce paper cups.

SERVINGS 8 (1 pop each)
CARB. PER SERVING 13 g
PREP 25 minutes **FREEZE** 4 hours 45 minutes

1 4-serving-size package fat-free, sugar-free, reduced-calorie vanilla instant pudding mix

2 cups cold fat-free milk

1 teaspoon vanilla

1 cup frozen light whipped dessert topping, thawed

8 5-ounce paper cups

1 cup fresh or thawed frozen strawberries

2 tablespoons sugar*

1 teaspoon lime juice

2 tablespoons snipped fresh basil

8 flat wooden crafts sticks

1 In a medium bowl combine pudding mix, milk, and vanilla; whisk for 2 to 3 minutes or until thickened. Fold in whipped topping. Pour ¼ cup of the pudding mixture into each of the paper cups, filling about one-third full; set aside the remaining pudding mixture. Tap each cup onto a countertop several times to help settle mixture into an even layer. Freeze about 15 minutes or until layer begins to set.

2 Meanwhile, in a food processor or blender combine strawberries, sugar, and lime juice. Cover and process or blend until smooth. Stir in basil.

3 Spoon about 1½ tablespoons of the strawberry-basil mixture evenly over pudding layer in each cup. Freeze about 30 minutes more or until firm.

4 Divide the remaining pudding mixture among the paper cups. Insert a crafts stick into each one. Freeze 4 to 24 hours or until firm.

*SUGAR SUBSTITUTES: We do not recommend using a sugar substitute for this recipe.

13 grams carb.

PER SERVING: 72 cal., 1 g total fat (1 g sat. fat), 1 mg chol., 168 mg sodium, 13 g carb. (0 g fiber, 8 g sugars), 2 g pro. Exchanges: 1 starch.

Blackberry Frozen Yogurt with Toasted Almonds and Waffle Wedges

Toasted frozen multigrain waffles fill in as a healthful, nonsweet substitute to classic sweet waffle cone pieces.

SERVINGS 6 ($\frac{1}{2}$ cup frozen yogurt, 3 waffle wedges, and 2 teaspoons almonds each)
CARB. PER SERVING 32 g
PREP 30 minutes CHILL 4 hours FREEZE time in ice cream maker + 2 hours
STAND 5 minutes

4 cups fresh blackberries

2 tablespoons water

1 6-ounce carton plain low-fat yogurt

$\frac{1}{4}$ cup honey

1 tablespoon snipped fresh mint

Butter-flavor nonstick cooking spray

$\frac{1}{4}$ cup slivered almonds

$\frac{1}{8}$ teaspoon ground cinnamon

$\frac{1}{8}$ teaspoon ground ginger

3 frozen round multigrain waffles, toasted

Fresh blackberries (optional)

Small fresh mint leaves (optional)

1 In a medium saucepan combine the 4 cups blackberries and the water. Bring to boiling; reduce heat. Simmer, covered, for 4 to 5 minutes or just until berries are softened and color turns to a bright maroon, stirring occasionally. Remove from the heat; cool slightly.

2 Pour blackberry mixture into a blender or food processor; cover and blend or process until smooth. Press pureed berries through a fine-mesh sieve; discard seeds. In a medium bowl whisk together strained berries, yogurt, honey, and snipped mint. Cover and chill for at least 4 hours or up to 24 hours.

3 Freeze the yogurt mixture in a $1\frac{1}{2}$-quart ice cream maker according to the manufacturer's directions. Transfer to an airtight container; cover. Freeze for at least 2 hours or up to 4 hours before serving. Let stand at room temperature 5 minutes before serving.

4 Meanwhile, coat an unheated small skillet with cooking spray. Add almonds; spread to an even layer. Coat almonds lightly with cooking spray. Sprinkle with cinnamon and ginger. Toss to coat. Cook over medium heat for 3 to 4 minutes or just until almonds are toasted, stirring often. Remove from heat; cool completely.

5 Cut each toasted waffle into six wedges. To serve, scoop frozen yogurt evenly into six serving bowls. Add three waffle wedges to each bowl. Sprinkle with almonds. If desired, garnish with additional blackberries and mint leaves.

PER SERVING: 173 cal., 5 g total fat (1 g sat. fat), 2 mg chol., 102 mg sodium, 32 g carb. (7 g fiber, 19 g sugars), 5 g pro. **Exchanges:** 0.5 fruit, 1 carb., 1 lean meat, 1 fat.

Neapolitan Frozen Mousse

Similar to the classic layered ice cream, this frosty dessert is easier to make than it looks.

SERVINGS 10 (1 slice each)
CARB. PER SERVING 22 g or 21 g
PREP 20 minutes
FREEZE 4 hours 30 minutes

¼ cup powdered sugar*

2 tablespoons unsweetened cocoa powder

1 16-ounce container frozen light whipped dessert topping, thawed

1 teaspoon vanilla

1½ cups fresh or thawed frozen strawberries

1 tablespoon granulated sugar*

PER SERVING: 128 cal., 5 g total fat (5 g sat. fat), 0 mg chol., 1 mg sodium, 22 g carb. (1 g fiber, 10 g sugars), 0 g pro. Exchanges: 1.5 carb., 1 fat.

PER SERVING WITH SUBSTITUTE: Same as above, except 124 cal., 21 g carb. (9 g sugars).

1 Line an 8×4×2-inch loaf pan with a double layer of plastic wrap, leaving a 2-inch overhang on all sides.

2 In a large chilled bowl whisk together powdered sugar and cocoa powder. Add 1 cup of the whipped topping, whisking until well mixed. Add another 1 cup of the whipped topping; fold together until no white streaks remain. Pour the chocolate mixture into the prepared pan, smoothing surface. Freeze about 15 minutes or just until the layer begins to set up.

3 In a clean bowl fold the vanilla into another 2 cups of the whipped topping. Spread this mixture over the slightly frozen chocolate layer, smoothing the top. Freeze for 15 minutes more.

4 In a blender or food processor combine strawberries and granulated sugar. Cover and blend or process until well mixed. Fold the strawberry mixture into the remaining whipped topping; spread over the vanilla layer. Loosely cover with the overhanging plastic wrap. Freeze for at least 4 hours or up to 24 hours or until firm.

5 To serve, use the edges of the plastic wrap to lift the mousse out of the pan and place on a cutting board. Remove and discard plastic wrap. Using a thin sharp knife that's been dipped in hot water, slice mousse into 10 slices, each about ¾ inch thick. Wipe knife dry after each cut.

*SUGAR SUBSTITUTES: We do not recommend using a sugar substitute for the powdered sugar. Choose Splenda Granular to substitute for the granulated sugar. Follow package directions to use product amount equivalent to 1 tablespoon granulated sugar.

Crepe Cake with Plums

Plums are in season May through early October. If you want to make this delicate dessert during the off-season, try fresh mangoes.

SERVINGS 16 (1 wedge each)
CARB. PER SERVING 21 g
PREP 25 minutes **CHILL** 3 hours

1½ pounds ripe yet firm red plums, pitted and very thinly sliced

¼ teaspoon ground cardamom

2 8-ounce containers frozen fat-free whipped dessert topping, thawed

½ teaspoon vanilla

10 9-inch purchased prepared crepes

1 tablespoon honey

1 Sprinkle plums with the cardamom. In a large bowl fold together whipped topping and vanilla.

2 To assemble the crepe cake, place one crepe on a serving platter; spread with about ½ cup of the whipped topping mixture and top with about ⅓ cup of the sliced plums. Repeat layering crepes, topping mixture, and plums until all the crepes, topping mixture, and plums are used. Cover and chill for at least 3 hours or up to 24 hours before serving.

3 To serve, drizzle with honey. Use a long serrated knife to cut cake into 16 wedges.

PER SERVING: 102 cal., 1 g total fat (0 g sat. fat), 4 mg chol., 65 mg sodium, 21 g carb. (1 g fiber, 8 g sugars), 1 g pro. Exchanges: 1 starch, 0.5 carb..

1 gram fat

QUICK TIP
Use a mandoline to get very thin plum slices. Set the mandoline just slightly thicker than ⅛ inch.

Panna Cotta with Mango Gelee

The key to making these layered puddinglike desserts is letting each layer set before adding the next.

SERVINGS 6 ($^{2}/_{3}$ cup each)
CARB. PER SERVING 24 g or 13 g
PREP 30 minutes STAND 10 minutes
CHILL 2 hours 15 minutes

4 teaspoons unflavored gelatin
3 tablespoons cold water
$2^{1}/_{4}$ cups low-fat (1%) milk
6 tablespoons sugar*
1 6-ounce carton plain fat-free or low-fat Greek yogurt
1 teaspoon vanilla
1 tablespoon cold water
1 cup cubed fresh or jarred mango (8 ounces)
1 teaspoon lime juice
$^{1}/_{4}$ cup water
Small lemon wedges (optional)
Small mango slices (optional)

PER SERVING: 127 cal., 1 g total fat (1 g sat. fat), 5 mg chol., 63 mg sodium, 24 g carb. (0 g fiber, 23 g sugars), 7 g pro. Exchanges: 1 milk, 1 carb..

PER SERVING WITH SUBSTITUTE: Same as above, except 85 cal., 13 g carb. (12 g sugars). Exchanges: 0 carb.

1 In a small bowl sprinkle 3 teaspoons of the gelatin over the 3 tablespoons cold water. Let stand about 5 minutes or until water is absorbed and gelatin is soft.

2 In a medium saucepan combine $^{1}/_{2}$ cup of the milk and 4 tablespoons of the sugar. Cook and stir over medium heat until sugar is dissolved and steam begins to rise. Remove from the heat. Add the softened gelatin; whisk until melted. Cool slightly. Whisk in the remaining $1^{3}/_{4}$ cups milk, the yogurt, and vanilla. Pour $^{1}/_{4}$ cup of the yogurt mixture into each of six 6-ounce dessert glasses. Set the remaining yogurt mixture aside and let stand at room temperature. Chill the mixture in glasses about 45 minutes or just until set.

3 Sprinkle the remaining 1 teaspoon gelatin over the 1 tablespoon cold water. Let stand for 5 minutes or until gelatin is soft. In a blender combine mango, lime juice, the remaining 2 tablespoons sugar, and $^{1}/_{4}$ cup water. Cover; blend until smooth. Transfer to a saucepan; warm over medium heat. Remove from heat. Add softened gelatin; whisk until melted.

4 Spoon 2 tablespoons mango mixture in each glass. Chill for 45 minutes or until mango mixture is set. Whisk reserved yogurt mixture until smooth. Divide among chilled glasses. Chill about 45 minutes or until layer is set. If desired, garnish with lemon wedges and additional small mango slices.

*SUGAR SUBSTITUTES: Choose from Splenda Granular, Truvia Spoonable, or Sweet'N Low bulk or packets. Follow directions to use product amount equivalent to 6 tablespoons sugar.

Island Tiramisu

Angel food cake takes the place of the classic, but sometimes-hard-to-find lady fingers in this tropical version of an Italian favorite.

SERVINGS 12 (1 piece each)
CARB. PER SERVING 22 g
PREP 25 minutes CHILL 8 hours

- 1 4-serving-size package fat-free, sugar-free, reduced-calorie banana cream instant pudding mix
- 1 cup cold fat-free milk
- 2 cups thawed frozen light whipped dessert topping
- $\frac{1}{3}$ cup chopped fresh pineapple
- $\frac{1}{3}$ cup chopped banana
- 1 small kiwifruit, peeled, quartered lengthwise, and sliced
- 1 teaspoon lime juice
- 9 ounces purchased angel food cake, cut into $\frac{1}{2}$-inch-thick slices
- $\frac{1}{4}$ cup shredded coconut, toasted

Chopped fresh pineapple and/or kiwifruit (optional)

Large coconut flakes, toasted (optional)

PER SERVING: 113 cal., 2 g total fat (2 g sat. fat), 0 mg chol., 258 mg sodium, 22 g carb. (1 g fiber, 11 g sugars), 2 g pro. Exchanges: 0.5 starch, 1 carb., 0.5 fat.

1 | In a medium bowl whisk together pudding mix and milk; fold in dessert topping. Set aside.

2 | In another medium bowl combine the $\frac{1}{3}$ cup pineapple, the banana, sliced kiwifruit, and lime juice; toss to coat.

3 | In a 2-quart square baking dish or 2-quart soufflé dish arrange half of the cake slices to cover the bottom of the dish. Spread half of the pudding mixture over the cake; sprinkle the fruit mixture over the pudding mixture.

4 | Arrange the remaining cake over the fruit mixture. Spread the remaining pudding mixture over all. Sprinkle with the $\frac{1}{4}$ cup toasted coconut. Cover and chill for at least 8 hours or up to 24 hours. If desired, garnish with additional chopped pineapple and/or kiwifruit and large coconut flakes.

Grilled Apricot Dessert Pizza

Try a different topping—top with berries instead of the kiwifruit, apricot, and plum.

SERVINGS 4 (¹/₄ of a flatbread with toppings each)
CARB. PER SERVING 23 g
PREP 15 minutes   GRILL 4 minutes

- 2 tablespoons reduced-fat cream cheese (Neufchâtel), softened
- 1 tablespoon sugar-free apricot preserves
- 1 rosemary-and-olive oil-flavor artisan pizza flatbread, such as Flatout brand
- 1 small apricot (2 ounces), pitted and thinly sliced
- 1 small kiwifruit (2 ounces), peeled and thinly sliced
- 1 small plum (2 ounces), pitted and thinly sliced
- 2 tablespoons sliced almonds, toasted
- 2 tablespoons honey
- 1 tablespoon finely snipped fresh mint (optional)

1 | In a small microwave-safe bowl combine cream cheese and preserves. Microwave, uncovered, on 100 percent power (high) for 15 seconds. Whisk to combine; set aside.

2 | For a charcoal or gas grill, grill flatbread on the rack of a covered grill directly over medium heat for 1 to 2 minutes or until bottom is lightly browned. Remove flatbread from grill. Spread cream cheese mixture evenly over browned side of flatbread. Top with apricot slices, kiwifruit slices, and plum slices. Return to grill. Cover and grill for 3 to 4 minutes more or until heated through and bottom of flatbread is toasted.

3 | Top with sliced almonds, drizzle with honey, and, if desired, sprinkle with mint.

3 grams pro.

PER SERVING: 127 cal., 3 g total fat (1 g sat. fat), 5 mg chol., 89 mg sodium, 23 g carb. (2 g fiber, 13 g sugars), 3 g pro. Exchanges: 0.5 fruit, 0.5 starch, 0.5 carb., 0.5 fat.

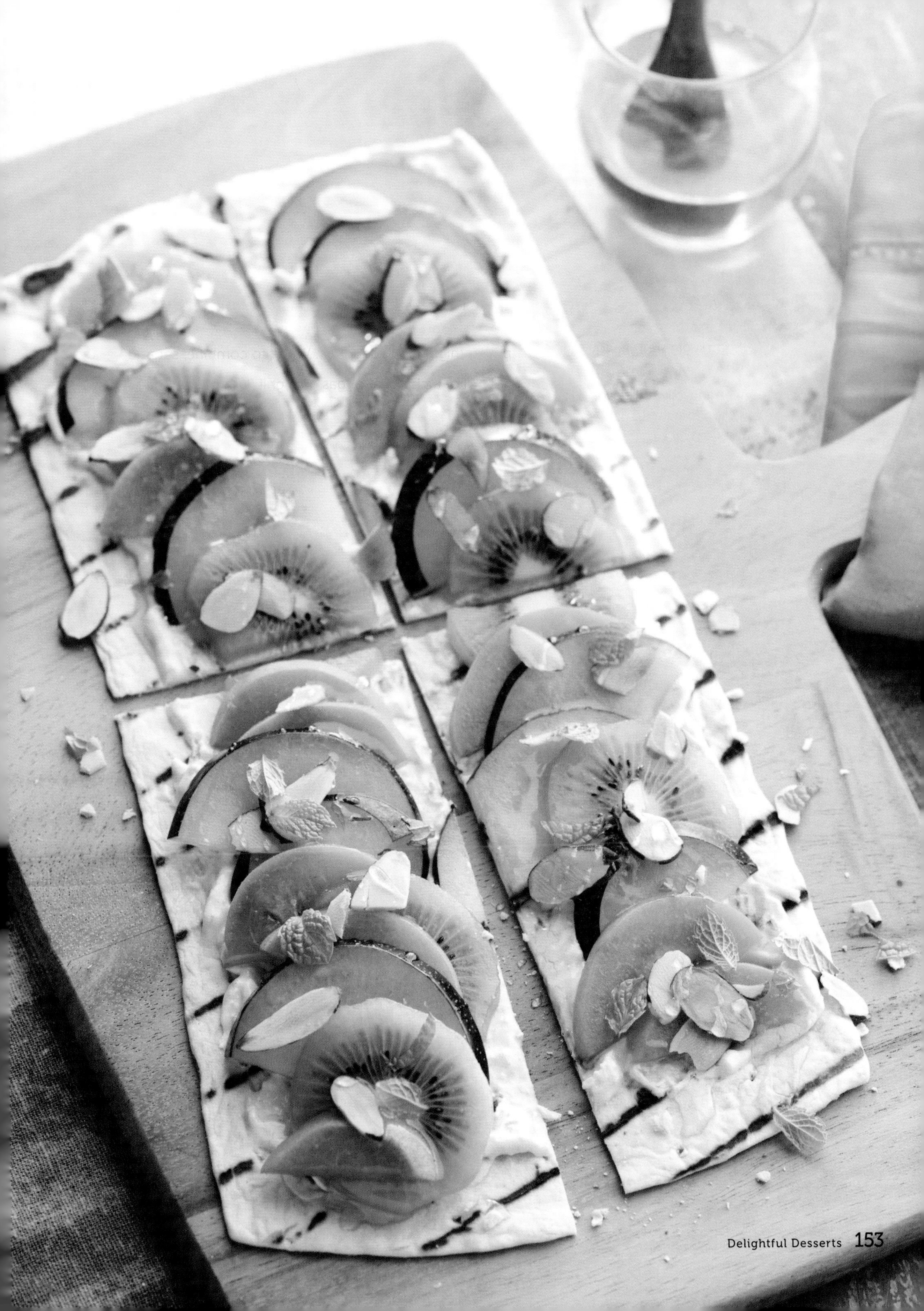

recipe index

recipe guide

See how we calculate nutrition information to help you count calories, carbs, and serving sizes.

Inside Our Recipes

Precise serving sizes (listed below the recipe title) help you to manage portions.

Ingredients listed as optional are not included in the per-serving nutrition analysis.

When kitchen basics such as ice, salt, black pepper, and nonstick cooking spray are not listed in the ingredients list, they are italicized in the directions.

Ingredients

• Tub-style vegetable oil spread refers to 60% to 70% vegetable oil product.

• Lean ground beef refers to 95% or leaner ground beef.

Nutrition Information

Nutrition facts per serving and food exchanges are noted with each recipe.

Test Kitchen tips and sugar substitutes are listed after the recipe directions.

When ingredient choices appear, we use the first one to calculate the nutrition analysis.

Key to Abbreviations

cal. = calories
sat. fat = saturated fat
chol. = cholesterol
carb. = carbohydrate
pro. = protein

metric information

The charts on this page provide a guide for converting measurements from the U.S. customary system, which is used throughout this book, to the metric system.

Product Differences

Most of the ingredients called for in the recipes in this book are available in most countries. However, some are known by different names. Here are some common American ingredients and their possible counterparts:

* All-purpose flour is enriched, bleached or unbleached white household flour. When self-rising flour is used in place of all-purpose flour in a recipe that calls for leavening, omit the leavening agent (baking soda or baking powder) and salt.
* Baking soda is bicarbonate of soda.
* Cornstarch is cornflour.
* Golden raisins are sultanas.
* Light-color corn syrup is golden syrup.
* Powdered sugar is icing sugar.
* Sugar (white) is granulated, fine granulated, or castor sugar.
* Vanilla or vanilla extract is vanilla essence.

Volume and Weight

The United States traditionally uses cup measures for liquid and solid ingredients. The chart below shows the approximate imperial and metric equivalents. If you are accustomed to weighing solid ingredients, the following approximate equivalents will be helpful.

* 1 cup butter, castor sugar, or rice = 8 ounces = $\frac{1}{2}$ pound = 250 grams
* 1 cup flour = 4 ounces = $\frac{1}{4}$ pound = 125 grams
* 1 cup icing sugar = 5 ounces = 150 grams

Canadian and U.S. volume for a cup measure is 8 fluid ounces (237 ml), but the standard metric equivalent is 250 ml.

1 British imperial cup is 10 fluid ounces.

In Australia, 1 tablespoon equals 20 ml, and there are 4 teaspoons in the Australian tablespoon.

Spoon measures are used for smaller amounts of ingredients. Although the size of the tablespoon varies slightly in different countries, for practical purposes and for recipes in this book, a straight substitution is all that's necessary. Measurements made using cups or spoons always should be level unless stated otherwise.

Common Weight Range Replacements

Imperial / U.S.	Metric
$\frac{1}{2}$ ounce	15 g
1 ounce	25 g or 30 g
4 ounces ($\frac{1}{4}$ pound)	115 g or 125 g
8 ounces ($\frac{1}{2}$ pound)	225 g or 250 g
16 ounces (1 pound)	450 g or 500 g
$1\frac{1}{4}$ pounds	625 g
$1\frac{1}{2}$ pounds	750 g
2 pounds or $2\frac{1}{4}$ pounds	1,000 g or 1 Kg

Oven Temperature Equivalents

Fahrenheit Setting	Celsius Setting*	Gas Setting
300°F	150°C	Gas Mark 2 (very low)
325°F	160°C	Gas Mark 3 (low)
350°F	180°C	Gas Mark 4 (moderate)
375°F	190°C	Gas Mark 5 (moderate)
400°F	200°C	Gas Mark 6 (hot)
425°F	220°C	Gas Mark 7 (hot)
450°F	230°C	Gas Mark 8 (very hot)
475°F	240°C	Gas Mark 9 (very hot)
500°F	260°C	Gas Mark 10 (extremely hot)
Broil	Broil	Grill

Electric and gas ovens may be calibrated using celsius. However, for an electric oven, increase celsius setting 10 to 20 degrees when cooking above 160°C. For convection or forced air ovens (gas or electric), lower the temperature setting 25°F/10°C when cooking at all heat levels.

Baking Pan Sizes

Imperial / U.S.	Metric
9×1$\frac{1}{2}$-inch round cake pan	22- or 23×4-cm (1.5 L)
9×1$\frac{1}{2}$-inch pie plate	22- or 23×4-cm (1 L)
8×8×2-inch square cake pan	20×5-cm (2 L)
9×9×2-inch square cake pan	22- or 23×4.5-cm (2.5 L)
11×7×1$\frac{1}{2}$-inch baking pan	28×17×4-cm (2 L)
2-quart rectangular baking pan	30×19×4.5-cm (3 L)
13×9×2-inch baking pan	34×22×4.5-cm (3.5 L)
15×10×1-inch jelly roll pan	40×25×2-cm
9×5×3-inch loaf pan	23×13×8-cm (2 L)
2-quart casserole	2 L

U.S. / Standard Metric Equivalents

$\frac{1}{8}$ teaspoon = 0.5 ml	
$\frac{1}{4}$ teaspoon = 1 ml	
$\frac{1}{2}$ teaspoon = 2 ml	
1 teaspoon = 5 ml	
1 tablespoon = 15 ml	
2 tablespoons = 25 ml	
$\frac{1}{4}$ cup = 2 fluid ounces = 50 ml	
$\frac{1}{3}$ cup = 3 fluid ounces = 75 ml	
$\frac{1}{2}$ cup = 4 fluid ounces = 125 ml	
$\frac{2}{3}$ cup = 5 fluid ounces = 150 ml	
$\frac{3}{4}$ cup = 6 fluid ounces = 175 ml	
1 cup = 8 fluid ounces = 250 ml	
2 cups = 1 pint = 500 ml	
1 quart = 1 litre	